Valerie Lum
Jenise Addison

Ice Cream Happy Hour

50 Boozy Treats You Spike, Freeze and Serve

Ulysses
Press

Published by:
Ulysses Press
P.O. Box 3440
Berkeley, CA 94703
www.ulyssespress.com

ISBN: 978-1-56975-931-8
Library of Congress Catalog Number 2011922519

Printed in Canada by Transcontinental Printing

10 9 8 7 6 5 4 3 2 1

Acquisitions editor: Kelly Reed
Managing editor: Claire Chun
Editors: Lauren Harrison, Leslie Evans
Proofreader: Barbara Schultz
Interior photographs: © Judi Swinks Photography except pages 11–17 © Lily Chou
Cover photograph: © Judi Swinks Photography
Interior illustrations: sundae pages 33, 43, 55, 93, 111, 113, 128, 133, 136, 141 © klipart.pl/fotolia.com; parfait page 38 © KMT/fotolia.com; milk shake pages 58 and 81 33737821 craig_pearson/fotolia.com; float page 64 © G. NICOLSON/fotolia.com; coffee cup page 77 © Jut/fotolia.com
Design and layout: what!design @ whatweb.com

Distributed by Publishers Group West

CONTENTS

INTRODUCTION

I f you're reading this book we can safely assume two things:

You like ice cream.
You like spirits.

So do we. We'd like to say that the conception of this book came after a long night of pairing cocktails with desserts at our swanky restaurant in Manhattan. Sadly, the reality was not nearly as glamorous. Instead, it was on the floor of a cramped kitchen in a one-bedroom railroad in Brooklyn that the idea of alcohol-infused ice cream came to be.

Jenise and I had spent a long Saturday night at the boutique beer shop in Park Slope in Brooklyn where we work as cooks and sandwich assemblers. We had considered heading to our neighborhood bar after work around midnight, but thought better of it.

"Doesn't a root beer float sound good right about now?" I said.

"Root beer? Try chocolate stout float!" Jenise said.

We bought our chocolate stout and a pint of vanilla ice cream and headed to the closest of our apartments. The beer immediately went in the freezer for a quick chill before we poured it into frosty mugs with scoops of ice cream.

"That hits the spot," I said.

After a few more floats, we were sprawled on the kitchen floor, rubbing our tired feet. It was in this state that I said, "I wonder why they don't make beer ice cream?"

Jenise, a professionally trained pastry cook, of course knew about the Guinness chocolate stout ice cream recipes included in most modern ice cream cookbooks. "I bet we can make that," she said.

The next week, we were back in the tiny kitchen with an ice cream maker taking up all the counter space. Jenise had developed a recipe for the custard and had made it the night before. It sat in the fridge next to the bottle of Guinness Extra Stout. Soon we were eating a soft-serve Guinness chocolate stout ice cream.

"This is brilliant," I said.

"I think we can do more, though," said Jenise. "I think we can get more beer in this."

While eating our fresh, homemade Guinness chocolate stout ice cream, we were already trying to figure out how to improve the recipe. We realized that the high water content in the Guinness was naturally going to lead to an icier ice cream, no matter how much fat from heavy cream or egg yolks we used to stabilize it. After much thought, Jenise realized that while working in pastries, she had often used gelatin to stabilize delicate desserts such as custards and mousses. "It should keep the ice cream creamy," she said. "And it should give it a good texture."

For the next batch of chocolate stout ice cream, we used an entire bottle of the beer instead of just 1 cup. We haphazardly added the gelatin to the custard. The ice cream became softer and creamier. We knew we were onto something.

With the method of beer ice cream well on its way to perfection, it seemed only natural to move on to stronger, boozier heights. As anyone who has ever stored liquor in the freezer knows, 80-proof alcohol does not freeze in a standard freezer. Nevertheless, I decided to try making a caramel spiced rum ice cream using 80-proof alcohol.

For the first batch, I whisked ¼ cup spiced rum into the custard to see what would happen. The ice cream did churn, but it was a bit icy. I tried it again with 2 tablespoons more spiced-rum, and the custard never quite set up correctly. Something else was needed.

It was then that I remembered college, and the house parties where Jell-O shots ran aplenty. I realized gelatin, the very ingredient we used to counteract the iciness of water and stabilize a beer-heavy ice cream, could also solidify 80-proof alcohol.

The actual process of developing a method for incorporating alcohol with gelatin, and finally the ice cream custard, took a lot of trial and error. There were batches with unappetizing chunks of alcohol-laden gelatin; one batch wouldn't churn because the alcohol wasn't cold enough; another was so bad a tester said it tasted like the bottom of a leather boot. But all of these mistakes helped us come up with a good system. We figured out that we can fit an entire cup of 80-proof alcohol into 1 quart of ice cream and it will solidify beautifully. It will also get you tipsy after a few spoonfuls.

As we developed more and more recipes, our friends started suggesting flavor combinations. We got so many, they didn't all make it into the book. But this is where you, the at-home ice cream maker, come in.

You can develop your own flavors. All you have to do is look at some of our basic recipes and adjust them. You can also learn from our mistakes, so please heed the notes that are in these recipes. We know all cooks love finding shortcuts, but a few of these can ruin your ice cream.

And we have to emphasize patience! If your ice cream maker requires a churning bowl to be completely frozen, that means completely frozen. The same goes for chilling custards and syrups before churning. And some flavors don't taste their best straight out of the ice cream maker, so give them a few hours in the freezer to allow the flavors to come together.

The point is, you're the ice cream chef now. You can call the shots in your own kitchen and pour the shots in your own ice cream. Have fun, be safe—and don't scoop and drive.

—Valerie Lum

VARIATIONS

C ustomizing your cocktail-inspired ice creams is a lot easier than you may think. You can take a lot of our base flavors, such as vanilla, chocolate, lemon, pineapple, and orange, and mix and match with various liquors and liqueurs to make your own fabulous treats. Don't be afraid to make your own boozy cocktail creations. After all, it's ice cream and liquor—how bad can it be?

The Proof is in the Custard: The ice cream recipes in this book have been spiked with beer, wine, liqueurs, and a variety of hard alcohols up to 80 proof, including vodka, rum, gin, and tequila, among others. For recipes using one of these hard alcohols, we found that ½ packet (½ tablespoon) of gelatin was sufficient for an ice cream batch containing ½ cup of 80-proof alcohol set up nicely. For the recipes that call for ⅔ to 1 cup of alcohol, it's best to use the full packet (1 tablespoon) of gelatin to stabilize the ice cream.

Any of the recipes in this book can be made with more or less booze, as long as you adjust the amount of gelatin accordingly. For some recipes, we felt ½ cup of liquor was sufficient to give the ice cream a solid booze flavor, while other recipes seemed to taste better with ¾ cup of the hard stuff. Feel free to adjust and experiment to get just the right amount of booziness for your palate or the occasion when the ice cream is being served.

The Phantom Punch: If you want a really strong alcohol flavor, you can always take a cup of the liquor you're using and reduce it down to between ¼ and ½ cup. Whisk the reduced liquor into the custard and use another cup of unreduced liquor to mix with the gelatin and spike the entire custard. Use this reduction technique with caution when incorporating sweet liqueurs such as amaretto. Otherwise, the flavor may become overwhelming in the ice cream.

BASIC SPIKED ICE CREAM TECHNIQUE

Scald the milk, cream, and sugar.

1 Mix the milk, heavy cream, and sugar in a medium saucepan over medium-low heat until the sugar is dissolved. Continue heating until the mixture is steamy and makes a slight sizzling noise when you move the pan. This is called scalding.

Note: Scalding does not mean simmering. Overheating the milk may cause curdling.

Whisk the egg yolks and temper.

1 While the milk mixture heats to scalding, whisk together the egg yolks in a medium bowl until they're light in color and slightly fluffy.

2. Gently stream about one-third of the hot milk mixture into the eggs while whisking continuously. This is called tempering. It's important to whisk while streaming the hot milk. If you just pour in the hot milk and then whisk, you may get scrambled eggs.

Thicken the custard.

1. Pour the egg and milk mixture into the rest of the milk mixture in the saucepan and stir continuously on low heat with a heatproof spatula or flat-ended wooden spoon. Make sure you scrape the bottom evenly while you continuously stir.

2. The custard is thick enough when you can draw a line on the back of the spoon with your finger and the line retains its shape. Note: If you have health concerns regarding eggs, you can check the temperature using an instant-read thermometer inserted into the middle of the custard. According to the Egg Safety Center, the minimum temperature should be 160°F (www.eggsafety.org/consumers/egg-safety).

Strain, cover, and chill the custard.

custard and none of it is exposed to air. This prevents a skin from developing.

1 Strain the custard through a fine-mesh strainer into a heatproof container.

3. Transfer the container to an ice bath and let it cool for about 30 minutes to stop the cooking process. Note: For sorbets and sherbets, no ice bath is required unless otherwise noted.

4. Transfer the container to the refrigerator. Chill until the custard is completely cold, at least 8 hours. Note: For many sorbets and sherbets, only 4 hours of chilling is required.

2. Cover with plastic wrap so that it's directly touching the entire surface of the

Dissolve the gelatin.

1. When the custard is cold and you're ready to churn the ice cream, dissolve the gelatin. Pour the water into a small saucepan or microwave-safe container and evenly sprinkle the gelatin on top.

2. Allow to sit until the gelatin appears to have absorbed as much water as it can, about 2 minutes. This is called blooming.

3. Gently warm over low heat and stir until the gelatin is completely dissolved into the liquid, about 3 minutes. If using a microwave, heat on medium power and check every 30 seconds until the gelatin is completely dissolved. The total time will depend on the microwave's voltage.

Note: It's important that the gelatin gets completely dissolved at this stage. Once the alcohol is mixed in, the gelatin denatures and will never fully dissolve. However, once the alcohol is added, clumps may form. This is fine since, in most cases, you strain the gelatin mixture before adding it to the custard. Do not try to reheat the gelatin mixture once you've added the alcohol; this will only denature the gelatin further, making it unable to solidify the ice cream, and it will also cook off the alcohol.

Spike the custard.

1 Refrigerate the alcohol until completely cold. Do not speed up the process by putting it in the freezer, which may make the gelatin set up too much before it is added to the custard.

2. Pour the gelatin into a medium bowl and whisk in the cold alcohol until combined. (Note: A recipe may contain more than one kind of alcohol.) Do not attempt to skip this step by pouring the alcohol directly into the saucepan or microwave-safe container with the gelatin. There might be enough residual heat to heat up the custard and prevent it from thickening in the ice cream maker (we learned this the hard way).

3. Pour the cold custard into a large bowl. Stream the alcohol and gelatin mixture through a fine-mesh strainer into the custard and whisk until thoroughly blended.

Churn the ice cream.

1 Pour the cold custard immediately into the ice cream maker and churn for at least 20 minutes, or as directed. Due to the alcohol content, you may wish to churn it longer to get the desired thickness. If you don't want to serve the ice cream immediately, or you want a firmer texture, transfer it to a freezer-proof container and freeze for several hours before serving.

BOOZY
ICE CREAMS

VANILLA WITH BRANDY

ICE CREAM   *This recipe proves that vanilla doesn't have to be boring. The classic flavor gets wonderful warmth from a heavy dose of brandy, which pairs well with alcohol-spiked fruit or cake. This was one of the first flavors we tinkered with, and we believe it's also a good starter flavor for the first-time spiked ice cream maker.*

1½ cups milk

1½ cups heavy cream

¾ cup sugar

1 vanilla bean

4 egg yolks

2 teaspoons vanilla extract

½ packet (½ tablespoon) gelatin

⅓ cup cold water

½ cup cold (refrigerated) brandy

MAKES ABOUT 1 QUART

1 Scald the milk, cream, and sugar with the vanilla bean. See page 11. While the milk mixture is heating, split the vanilla bean down the center lengthwise and scrape out the seeds. Whisk the seeds into the milk mixture, then add the empty pod to the pan.

2. Steep the milk mixture and vanilla. Once the milk mixture is scalding, remove the pan from the heat and cover it. After about 30 minutes, remove the vanilla bean pod and set it aside.

3. Reheat the milk mixture back up to scalding.

4. Whisk the egg yolks and temper with one-third of the scalding milk mixture. See page 12.

5. **Thicken the custard** over low heat. See page 13.

6. **Whisk in the vanilla extract.**

7. **Strain, cover, and chill the custard** for at least 8 hours. See page 14. Add the empty vanilla bean pod to the custard before covering it.

Once the custard is completely cold...

8. **Remove the vanilla bean** pod from the custard.

9. **Dissolve the gelatin** in the cold water. See page 15.

10. **Spike the custard** with the cold brandy and gelatin mixture. See page 16.

11. **Churn the ice cream** for at least 20 minutes. See page 17.

Variations

VANILLA WITH VODKA: Omit the brandy and substitute with vodka.

VANILLA WITH BOURBON: Omit the brandy and substitute with bourbon.

CHOCOLATE WITH GRAND MARNIER

ICE CREAM   *Dark chocolate and orange liqueur make for a creamy, luscious ice cream. Some may call it a tired combination, but it's still delicious and almost downright addictive. Chocolate lovers rejoice!*

1½ cups milk

1½ cups heavy cream

½ cup sugar

1 teaspoon vanilla extract

grated zest of 1 orange

4 egg yolks

6 ounces dark chocolate, chopped, or dark chocolate chips

½ packet (½ tablespoon) gelatin

⅓ cup cold water

½ cup cold (refrigerated) Grand Marnier

MAKES ABOUT 1 QUART

1 Scald the milk, cream, and sugar and the vanilla extract and orange zest. See page 11.

2. Steep the milk mixture and zest. Once the milk is scalding, remove the pan from the heat and cover it. After 15 minutes, strain out the zest.

3. Reheat the milk mixture back up to scalding.

4. Whisk the egg yolks and temper with one-third of the scalding milk mixture. See page 12.

5. Thicken the custard over low heat. See page 13.

6. Melt the chocolate. Place the chocolate into a large heatproof bowl with a fine-mesh strainer on top. Pour the hot custard through the strainer into the chocolate. Stir until the chocolate is completely melted.

7. Cover and chill the custard for at least 8 hours. See page 14.

Once the custard is completely cold...

8. Dissolve the gelatin in the cold water. See page 15.

9. Spike the custard with the cold Grand Marnier and gelatin mixture. See page 16.

10. Churn the ice cream for at least 20 minutes. See page 17.

Variation

CHOCOLATE WITH IRISH WHISKEY: Omit the Grand Marnier and orange zest. Substitute ¾ cup of Irish whiskey and increase the gelatin to 1 full packet (1 tablespoon).

STRAWBERRY WITH VODKA

ICE CREAM   *Although strawberry ice cream is unquestionably a wholesome, classic flavor, the inspiration for this recipe actually came from a bar in Chico, California. It was there that a bar called Riley's served strawberry smoothie shots made with strawberry puree, whipped cream, vodka, and triple sec. Many a long night was fueled with those sweet little shots, and here they get a grown-up update.*

1 pound strawberries, hulled and quartered

¾ cup sugar, divided

2 tablespoons vodka plus ¼ cup cold vodka, divided

1¼ cups milk

1¼ cups heavy cream

2 egg yolks

½ packet (½ tablespoon) gelatin

⅓ cup cold water

¼ cup cold (refrigerated) triple sec

MAKES ABOUT 1 QUART

1 Macerate the strawberries by tossing them in a medium bowl with ¼ cup sugar and 2 tablespoons vodka. Allow to sit at room temperature for 1 hour.

2. Puree the macerated strawberries in a blender or food processor, then strain through a fine-mesh strainer and discard the seeds.

3. Reduce the strawberry puree in a small saucepan over low heat. Simmer the puree until it reduces down to a little more than 1 cup and reaches a jamlike consistency, about 30 minutes. Pour into a large heatproof bowl and set aside.

4. Scald the milk, cream, and sugar using the remaining ½ cup sugar. See page 11.

5. Whisk the egg yolks and temper with one-third of the scalding milk mixture. See page 12.

6. Thicken the custard over low heat. See page 13.

7. Strain, cover, and chill the custard. Strain the custard into the strawberry puree and whisk until combined. Refrigerate the custard for at least 8 hours. See page 14.

Once the custard is completely cold...

8. Dissolve the gelatin in the cold water. See page 15.

9. Spike the custard with the cold ½ cup vodka, triple sec, and gelatin mixture. See page 16.

10. Churn the ice cream for at least 20 minutes. See page 17. Don't strain the custard; pour it directly into the ice cream maker.

CHERRY VANILLA WITH BRANDY

ICE CREAM   *This ice cream requires quick brandied cherries, so it takes a little planning ahead of time, but the bursts of brandied cherries with vanilla cherry ice cream are definitely worth the time and effort. We used about 14 ounces of cherries, which measured out to about 2 cups. You can use a little less or a little more; just make sure you divide the entire amount in half, one half for brandied cherries and the other for the puree.*

2 cups sweet cherries (about 14 ounces), stemmed, divided

¾ cup plus 3 tablespoons sugar, divided

1½ cups brandy, or enough to cover half the cherries

1½ cups milk

1½ cups heavy cream

1 vanilla bean

pinch of salt

4 egg yolks

1 packet (1 tablespoon) gelatin

⅓ cup cold water

MAKES ABOUT 1 QUART

1 **Soak half the cherries in brandy** by quartering and removing the pits from about 1 cup of cherries. Place them in a medium jar. Add 3 tablespoons sugar and enough brandy to cover the cherries. Cover the jar and mix well. Refrigerate the brandied cherries for at least 48 hours, or up to a week (any longer and you risk the cherries getting too squishy).

When the brandied cherries are drunk enough for your liking...

2. **Puree the fresh cherries.** Remove the pits from the remaining 1 cup

cherries and puree the fruit in a food processor or blender. Transfer to a large heatproof bowl and set aside.

3. Scald the milk, cream, and sugar with the vanilla bean and salt, using the remaining ¾ cup sugar. See page 11. While the milk mixture is heating, split the vanilla bean down the center lengthwise and scrape out the seeds. Whisk the seeds into the milk mixture, then add the empty pod to the pan.

4. Steep the milk mixture and vanilla. Once the milk mixture is scalding, remove the pan from the heat and cover it. After about 30 minutes, remove the vanilla bean pod and set it aside.

5. Reheat the milk mixture back up to scalding.

6. Whisk the egg yolks and temper with one-third of the scalding milk mixture. See page 12.

7. Thicken the custard over low heat. See page 13.

8. Strain, cover, and chill the custard. Strain the custard into the heatproof bowl with the cherry puree and stir well, and refrigerate for at least 8 hours. See page 14. Add the empty vanilla bean pod to the custard before covering it.

Once the custard is completely cold...

9. Drain the brandied cherries and reserve the liquid. Allow to drain for about 10 minutes.

10. Remove the vanilla bean pod from the custard.

11. Dissolve the gelatin in the cold water. See page 15.

12. Spike the custard with 6 tablespoons of the reserved cherry brandy whisked into the gelatin. See page 16.

13. Churn the ice cream. Don't strain the custard; pour it directly into the ice cream maker and churn for about 15 minutes. Once the ice cream appears to be just a little too fluffy, add the brandied cherries to the mixer and churn again until the ice cream thickens, about 5 minutes more. If the cherries aren't mixed in enough by the time the ice cream is finished churning, you can remove the paddle and gently fold them in by hand while they're still in the freezer bowl. If you don't want to serve the ice cream immediately, or you want a firmer texture, transfer it to a freezer-proof container and freeze for several hours before serving.

COOKIES AND CREAM WITH VODKA

ICE CREAM *You may be an adult now, with adult taste buds, but that doesn't mean you can't still enjoy a good cookie-filled ice cream. Think of it as a way to celebrate your adulthood and enjoy your milk and cookies, too.*

1½ cups milk

1½ cups heavy cream

¾ cup sugar

1 vanilla bean

4 egg yolks

2 teaspoons vanilla extract

½ packet (½ tablespoon) gelatin

⅓ cup cold water

½ cup cold (refrigerated) vodka

5 to 6 chocolate sandwich cookies, crumbled

MAKES ABOUT 1 QUART

1 Scald the milk, cream, and sugar with the vanilla bean. See page 11. While the milk mixture is heating, split the vanilla bean down the center lengthwise and scrape out the seeds. Whisk the seeds into the milk mixture, then add the empty pod to the pan.

2. Steep the milk mixture and vanilla. Once the milk mixture is scalding, remove the pan from the heat and cover it. After about 30 minutes, remove the vanilla bean pod and set it aside.

3. Reheat the milk mixture back up to scalding.

4. Whisk the egg yolks and temper with one-third of the scalding milk mixture. See page 12.

5. **Thicken the custard** over low heat. See page 13.

6. **Whisk in the vanilla extract.**

7. **Strain, cover, and chill the custard** for at least 8 hours. See page 14. Add the empty vanilla bean pod to the custard before covering it.

Once the custard is completely cold...

8. **Remove the vanilla bean pod** from the custard.

9. **Dissolve the gelatin** in the cold water. See page 15.

10. **Spike the custard** with the cold vodka and gelatin mixture. See page 16.

11. **Churn the ice cream** for at least 20 minutes. See page 17. If you don't want to serve the ice cream immediately, don't put it in the freezer yet.

12. **Add the cookies.** Scoop about one-third of the custard into a large bowl and sprinkle about one-third of the crumbled cookies on top. Repeat the layers twice more with the remaining ice cream and cookies, then gently fold it all together. Be sure to work quickly—if the ice cream melts too much, it will just get icy once it's in the freezer.

If you don't want to serve the ice cream immediately, or you want a firmer texture, transfer the ice cream to a freezer-proof container and freeze for several hours before serving.

VODKA BANANA SPLIT

We're taking that good old-fashioned soda fountain treat and giving it a new twist.

Slice a banana lengthwise and lay the slices in the bottom of an oblong dish. Place 1 scoop Chocolate Martini ice cream (page 79), 1 scoop Vanilla with Vodka ice cream (page 21), and 1 scoop Strawberry with Vodka ice cream (page 25) on top of the banana. Spoon Vodka Strawberry Topping (page 128) over the chocolate ice cream, Whiskey Caramel Sauce (page 136) over the vanilla ice cream, and Chocolate Sauce (page 141) over the strawberry ice cream. Top each scoop with a dollop of Boozy Whipped Cream (page 133), and garnish with chopped peanuts and a Drunken Maraschino Cherry (page 113).

COFFEE WITH KAHLÚA

ICE CREAM   *This coffee liqueur has a fond place in our hearts because it's our grandparents' cocktail of choice. This recipe, unlike Irish Coffee (page 86), requires the beans to simmer in the milk mixture so their flavor is fully infused. This is also a key ingredient for a Mudslide Sundae (page 148).*

1½ cups milk

1½ cups heavy cream

1 cup sugar, divided

½ vanilla bean

1 cup whole coffee beans

4 egg yolks

1 packet (1 tablespoon) gelatin

½ cup water

½ cup cold (refrigerated) Kahlúa

MAKES ABOUT 1 QUART

1 Scald the milk, cream, and sugar with the vanilla bean using ½ cup sugar. See page 11. While the milk mixture is heating, split the vanilla bean down the center lengthwise and scrape out the seeds. Whisk the seeds into the milk mixture, then add the empty pod to the pan.

2. Steep the milk mixture and vanilla. Once the milk mixture is scalding, add the coffee beans. Remove the pan from the heat and cover. After about 15 minutes, strain out the coffee beans and discard. Remove the vanilla bean pod.

3. Return the milk mixture back up to scalding.

4. **Whisk the egg yolks and temper.** Whisk the egg yolks with the remaining ½ cup sugar and temper with one-third of the scalding milk mixture. See page 12.

5. **Thicken the custard** over low heat. See page 13.

6. **Strain, cover, and chill the custard** for at least 8 hours. See page 14.

Once the custard is completely cold...

7. **Dissolve the gelatin** in the cold water. See page 15.

8. **Spike the custard** with the cold Kahlúa and gelatin mixture. See page 16.

9. **Churn the ice cream** for at least 20 minutes. See page 17.

MINT CHIP WITH CRÈME DE MENTHE

ICE CREAM   *Mint chip ice cream gets a bit of a kick from crème de menthe. If you really want an eye-popping green color, like the ice creams you find in the grocery store, you might want to consider using food coloring.*

2 cups milk

2 cups heavy cream

¾ cup sugar

4 egg yolks

2 teaspoons mint extract

3 to 4 drops green food coloring (optional)

1 packet (1 tablespoon) gelatin

¼ cup cold water

¾ cup cold (refrigerated) crème de menthe

1 cup chopped chocolate

MAKES ABOUT 1 QUART

1. Scald the milk, cream, and sugar. See page 11.

2. Whisk the egg yolks and temper with one-third of the scalding milk mixture. See page 12.

3. **Thicken the custard** over low heat. See page 13.

4. **Whisk in the mint extract** and food coloring, if using.

5. **Strain, cover, and chill** the custard for least 8 hours. See page 14.

Once the custard is completely cold...

6. **Dissolve the gelatin** in the cold water. See page 15.

7. **Spike the custard** with the cold crème de menthe and gelatin mixture. See page 16.

8. **Churn the ice cream** for at least 20 minutes. See page 17.

9. **Add the chocolate.** Scoop about one-quarter of the ice cream into a freezer-proof container and sprinkle about one-quarter of the chopped chocolate on top. Repeat the layers three more times, then gently fold it all together. Be sure to work quickly—if the ice cream melts too much, it will just get icy once it's in the freezer.

WHITE RUSSIAN PARFAIT

This delicious concoction takes the classic White Russian to a whole new level. Walnuts seemed to us like the most natural nuts to sprinkle on top, but try pistachios for extra color.

Scoop White Russian ice cream (page 89) into the bottom of a tall glass to make a layer about 1 inch thick. Pour a thin layer of Chocolate Sauce (page 141) on top, then add a 1-inch layer of Coffee with Kahlúa ice cream (page 34). Continue alternating all three layers to the top of the glass. Top with Boozy Whipped Cream made with Bailey's Irish Cream (page 133) and chopped nuts like walnuts, pistachios, or pecans.

ORANGE SHERBET WITH AMARETTO

Orange sherbet has always been a favorite of ours, so when an old friend introduced us to a drink mixing orange juice and amaretto, the idea of turning it into a sherbet immediately came to mind. Because it's a sherbet, this easy recipe has the advantage of having no eggs, so there's no need for cooking either.

1 cup sugar

2 cups fresh orange juice

1 tablespoon fresh lemon juice

1½ cups milk

1 teaspoon vanilla extract
or almond extract

1 packet (1 tablespoon) gelatin

⅓ cup cold water

¾ cup cold (refrigerated) amaretto

MAKES ABOUT 1 QUART

1 **Make the syrup.** In a medium bowl, whisk the sugar, orange juice, and lemon juice together until the sugar is completely dissolved.

2. **Whisk in the milk** and vanilla or almond extract.

3. **Cover and chill the syrup** for at least 4 hours. See page 14.

Once the syrup is completely cold...

4. **Dissolve the gelatin** in the cold water. See page 15.

5. **Spike the syrup** with the cold amaretto and gelatin mixture. See page 16.

6. **Churn the sherbet** for at least 20 minutes. See page 17.

ORANGE CRÈMESICLE WITH COINTREAU

ICE CREAM   *Get ready to flash back to your childhood ice cream truck days with this orange classic. This flavor gets a healthy kick of alcohol with the help of Cointreau and pisco. It's so sweet and citrusy, you'll forget you're not eating it off a stick.*

1½ cups milk

1½ cups heavy cream

1 cup sugar, divided

1 vanilla bean

2 egg yolks

1½ cups cold fresh orange juice, divided

½ packet (½ tablespoon) gelatin

¼ cup cold (refrigerated) Cointreau

¼ cup cold (refrigerated) pisco

MAKES ABOUT 1 QUART

1 Scald the milk, cream, and ½ cup sugar. See page 11. While the milk mixture is heating, split the vanilla bean down the center lengthwise and scrape out the seeds. Whisk the seeds into the milk mixture, then add the empty pod to the pan.

2. Steep the milk mixture and vanilla. Once the milk mixture is scalding, remove the pan from the heat and cover it. After about 30 minutes, remove the vanilla bean pod and set it aside.

3. Reheat the milk mixture back up to scalding.

4. Whisk the egg yolks and temper. Whisk the egg yolks with the remaining ½ cup sugar until light and fluffy and temper with one-third of the scalding milk mixture. See page 12.

5. Thicken the custard over low heat. See page 13.

6. Mix the custard with 1 cup cold orange juice in a medium bowl.

7. Strain, cover, and chill the custard for at least 8 hours. See page 14.

Once the custard is completely cold...

8. Dissolve the gelatin in the remaining ½ cup cold orange juice. See page 15.

9. Spike the custard with the cold Cointreau, pisco, and gelatin mixture. See page 16.

10. Churn the ice cream for at least 20 minutes. See page 17.

ROCKY ROAD WITH CRÈME DE CACAO

ICE CREAM   *Chocolate, marshmallow, and nuts—what more could you want? Crème de cacao was the natural choice for this ice cream, and it won't disappoint.*

2 cups milk

2 cups heavy cream

½ cup sugar

1 teaspoon vanilla extract

4 egg yolks

7 ounces dark chocolate, chopped, or dark chocolate chips

1 packet (1 tablespoon) gelatin

⅓ cup cold water

¾ cup cold (refrigerated) crème de cacao

½ cup chopped chocolate

½ cup mini marshmallows

½ cup chopped nuts, such as peanuts, almonds, pecans, or even pistachios

MAKES ABOUT 1 QUART

1 Scald the milk, cream, and sugar and the vanilla extract. See page 11.

2. Whisk the egg yolks and temper with one-third of the scalding milk mixture. See page 12.

3. Thicken the custard over low heat. See page 13.

4. Melt the chocolate. Place the chocolate in a large heatproof bowl with a fine-mesh strainer on top. Pour the hot custard through the strainer into the chocolate. Stir until the chocolate is completely melted.

5. Cover and chill the custard for at least 8 hours. See page 14.

Once the custard is completely cold...

6. Dissolve the gelatin in the cold water. See page 15.

9. Spike the custard with the cold crème de cacao and gelatin mixture. See page 16.

10. Churn the ice cream for at least 20 minutes. See page 17.

11. Add the chocolate, marshmallows, and nuts. Once the ice cream is churned, gently fold in the chocolate, marshmallows, and nuts. For a firmer texture, transfer it to a freezer-proof container and freeze for several hours before serving.

TURTLE SUNDAE

This is another classic with a kick.

Place 1 scoop Vanilla with Brandy ice cream (page 21) and 1 scoop Butter Pecan with Brandy ice cream (page 50) in a dish. Drizzle with Chocolate Sauce (page 141) and Whiskey Caramel Sauce (page 136). Top with a dollop of Boozy Whipped Cream made with brandy (page 133) and garnish with Candied Pecans (page 53).

80-PROOF SPECIALTIES

BUTTERED RUM

ICE CREAM   *The richness of butter and eggs mixed with the muskiness of dark rum gets even sexier with the addition of nutmeg. Ground nutmeg will do in a pinch, but for mind-blowing flavor, freshly grate the nutmeg right into the custard.*

¼ cup dark rum

¼ cup water

1 cup brown sugar

⅛ teaspoon salt

⅛ teaspoon freshly grated nutmeg

2 egg yolks

2 tablespoons butter, diced, at room temperature

1 cup milk

1 teaspoon vanilla extract

1 cup heavy cream

MAKES ABOUT 1 QUART

1. Make the rum syrup. Mix the rum, water, brown sugar, and salt in a small bowl and grate in the nutmeg. Stir to dissolve, and cook on low heat until it turns into a light syrup, about 2 minutes.

2. Whisk the egg yolks and temper. Whisk the egg yolks in a double boiler until fluffy. Turn the heat to low and slowly stream the rum syrup into the eggs while stirring gently.

3. Thicken the mixture. Gently cook the mixture over low heat while stirring continuously with a heatproof spatula or flat-ended wooden spoon. Turn off the heat when you can draw a line on the back of the spoon with your finger and the line retains its shape.

4. Stir in the butter.

5. **Strain, cover, and chill the custard** for at least 8 hours. See page 14.

Once the custard is completely cold...

6. **Pour the cold custard into a large bowl** and whisk in the milk and vanilla extract.

7. **Whisk the heavy cream**. In a medium bowl, whisk the heavy cream vigorously until it reaches soft peaks.

8. **Fold the whipped cream** into the custard.

9. **Churn the ice cream** for at least 20 minutes. See page 17.

CARAMEL WITH SPICED RUM

ICE CREAM   *This is not a beginner's ice cream. It involves caramelizing sugar, which can be tricky. Don't stir the sugar. When you stir it, sugar can get stuck to the side of the pan, where it will harden and turn into shards of sugar in the caramel. This recipe will also bubble up rapidly, so keep an eye on it at all times. Have all your ingredients and equipment ready within arm's reach so that you don't have to step away for a moment, when the bubble-overs like to hit.*

1½ cups milk

1½ cups heavy cream

¾ cup sugar

1 tablespoon butter, diced, at room temperature

4 egg yolks

½ packet (½ tablespoon) gelatin

⅓ cup cold water

½ cup cold (refrigerated) spiced rum

MAKES ABOUT 1 QUART

1 Scald the milk and cream; don't add the sugar yet. See page 11.

2. Caramelize the sugar. While the milk mixture is heating, place the sugar in an even layer in a small saucepan. Turn the heat to medium-high and resist the urge to stir the sugar. Once the edges start to liquefy, about 3 minutes, gently agitate the sugar with a wooden spoon, pulling the edges to the middle of the pan, until the sugar is evenly melted and deep amber in color, about 8 minutes. You want a deep caramel color. Note: If you stir the sugar before it starts to completely melt, you may cause shards of sugar to develop around the edges. Heating the sugar further may cause the sugar to burn too much.

3. Whisk in the butter. Add the butter to the deep amber sugar. Immediately start whisking, because the sugar will start rapidly bubbling. Continue whisking until the bubbling subsides.

4. Whisk in the milk mixture. Once the butter is fully incorporated into the sugar and the bubbling has ceased, continue whisking and stream in some of the scalded milk mixture. The sugar mixture will immediately bubble over, so continue whisking and adding the rest of the milk mixture until the bubbling subsides. Note: Since the juggling of pots might get a little tricky, you can add the milk mixture in phases. However, it's important to continue whisking evenly.

5. Transfer the milk and caramel mixture back to the medium saucepan over low heat and return to scalding.

6. Whisk the egg yolks and temper with one-third of the milk and caramel mixture. See page 12.

7. Thicken the custard over low heat. See page 13.

8. Strain, cover, and chill the custard for at least 8 hours. See page 14.

Once the custard is completely cold...

9. Dissolve the gelatin in the cold water. See page 15.

10. Spike the custard with the cold spiced rum and gelatin mixture. See page 16.

11. Churn the ice cream for at least 20 minutes. See page 17.

BUTTER PECAN WITH BRANDY

ICE CREAM   *This recipe calls for candied pecans; however, toasted pecan halves can be substituted if you don't have the time. We recommend going the extra mile though. It gives the pecans a great texture along with the flavor.*

1 cup milk

2 cups heavy cream

½ vanilla bean

4 egg yolks

⅔ cup brown sugar

2 teaspoons cornstarch

1 packet (1 tablespoon) gelatin

⅓ cup cold water

¼ cup cold (refrigerated) brandy

2 cups Candied Pecans (recipe follows)

MAKES ABOUT 1½ QUARTS

1 Scald the milk and cream with the vanilla bean; don't add the sugar yet. See page 11. While the milk mixture is heating, split the vanilla bean down the center lengthwise and scrape out the seeds. Whisk the seeds into the milk mixture, then add the empty pod to the pan.

2. Steep the milk mixture and vanilla. Once the milk mixture is scalding, remove the pan from the heat and cover it. After about 15 minutes, remove the vanilla bean pod.

3. Reheat the milk mixture back up to scalding.

4. Whisk the egg yolks and temper. Whisk the egg yolks with the brown sugar and cornstarch and temper with one-third of the scalding milk mixture. See page 12.

5. Thicken the custard over low heat. See page 13. The custard should thicken rather quickly because of the cornstarch.

6. Strain, cover, and chill the custard for at least 8 hours. See page 14.

Once the custard is completely cold...

7. Dissolve the gelatin in the cold water. See page 15.

8. Spike the custard with the cold brandy and gelatin mixture. See page 16.

9. Churn the ice cream for at least 20 minutes. See page 17. If you don't want to serve the ice cream immediately, don't put it in the freezer yet.

10. Add the candied pecans. Scoop about one-third of the ice cream into a freezer-proof container and sprinkle about one-third of the candied pecans on top. Repeat the layers twice more with the remaining ice cream and pecans, then gently fold it all together. Be sure to work quickly—if the ice cream melts too much, it will just get icy once it's in the freezer.

CANDIED PECANS

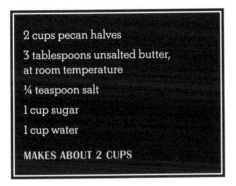

2 cups pecan halves

3 tablespoons unsalted butter, at room temperature

¼ teaspoon salt

1 cup sugar

1 cup water

MAKES ABOUT 2 CUPS

1. Toast the pecans. Preheat the oven to 350°F. Lay the pecans in a single layer on a rimmed baking sheet and toast in the oven until golden brown, about 10 minutes.

2. Season the pecans. Once the pecans are toasted, roll them in the butter and sprinkle with salt.

3. Melt the sugar. Put the sugar in a large saucepan. Add just enough water to the sugar until it is the texture of wet sand (you might not use all the water). Cook over low heat until the sugar is dissolved, about 5 minutes. Stir very gently; try not to get any sugar on the side of the pot.

4. Soft-crack the sugar. Once the sugar is completely dissolved, continue cooking until it is soft-cracked, about 15 minutes. At this point the sugar should be colorless but viscous, and the bubbles should be on the small side. You can also use a candy thermometer; the temperature should be between 270°F and 290°F.

5. Add the pecans. Remove the pan from the heat and add the toasted pecans. Tilt the pan at an angle and rapidly stir the pecans to aerate and evenly coat them with the sugar syrup.

6. Candy the pecans. Once the pecans are evenly coated, return the pan to the stove over low heat and periodically stir the pecans until they look like they're coated with crunchy caramel and white sugar, about 5 minutes.

7. Cool the pecans in a single layer on a baking sheet. Once they're completely cool, chop them.

MAPLE WITH BOURBON

ICE CREAM   *As a taste tester said of this recipe's surprisingly enticing flavor pairing, "This ice cream makes me want to get in a fight and eat some pancakes." A key component in our Nor'easter Float (page 153), this ice cream was inspired by the restaurant Char No. 4 in Brooklyn, where they use maple syrup in their version of the drink.*

¾ cup Grade B maple syrup

1½ cups milk

1½ cups heavy cream

2 tablespoons brown sugar

4 egg yolks

2 teaspoons molasses

2 tablespoons fresh lime juice

pinch of salt

½ packet (½ tablespoon) gelatin

⅓ cup cold water

½ cup cold (refrigerated) bourbon

MAKES ABOUT 1 QUART

1 Reduce the maple syrup. In a small saucepan, heat the maple syrup over medium heat. Simmer, uncovered, until reduced by half, about 15 minutes. Set aside and allow to cool.

2. Scald the milk, cream, and brown sugar. See page 11.

3. Whisk the egg yolks and temper with one-third of the scalding milk mixture. See page 12.

4. Thicken the custard over low heat. See page 13.

5. Whisk in the molasses, maple syrup reduction, lime juice, and salt.

7. **Strain, cover, and chill the custard** for at least 8 hours. See page 14.

Once the custard is completely cold...

8. **Dissolve the gelatin** in the cold water. See page 15.

9. **Spike the custard** with the cold bourbon and gelatin mixture. See page 16.

10. **Churn the ice cream** for at least 20 minutes. See page 17.

PIÑA COLADA SUNDAE

This is a simple sundae you can make to up your Piña Colada ice cream's presentation. When you're making the ice cream, toast some extra coconut for garnish. Serve this sundae in a piña colada glass—don't forget the paper umbrella!

Place 2 scoops Piña Colada ice cream (page 108) in a dish and top with Rum Pineapple Topping (page 111). Top with a dollop of Boozy Whipped Cream made with coconut rum (page 133), and garnish with toasted coconut shavings and a Drunken Maraschino Cherry (page 113).

JASMINE TEA WITH SAKE

SHERBET   *Blending the sweetness of sake with the floral headiness of jasmine is one of those amazing flavor combinations few people would have thought of. Luckily we did, because the complex flavors pair beautifully. Jasmine pearls are tea leaves that have been hand-rolled to look like pearl-size beads. You can find them at most tea shops and at some grocery stores.*

1½ cups milk

1½ cups heavy cream

½ cup sugar

5 tablespoons light corn syrup

¼ vanilla bean

2 tablespoons jasmine tea pearls

1 packet (1 tablespoon) gelatin

⅓ cup cold water

¾ cup cold (refrigerated) nigori sake

MAKES ABOUT 1 QUART

1 Scald the milk, cream, and sugar with the corn syrup. See page 11. While the milk mixture is heating, split the ¼ vanilla bean down the center lengthwise and scrape out the seeds. Whisk the seeds into the mixture, then add the empty pod to the pan.

2. **Steep the milk mixture, vanilla bean, and jasmine pearls.** Once the milk mixture is scalding, remove the pan from the heat. Add the jasmine pearls, cover the pan, and steep for about 15 minutes.

3. **Strain, cover, and chill the mixture** for at least 8 hours. See page 14.

Once the mixture is completely cold...

4. **Dissolve the gelatin** in the cold water. See page 15.

5. **Spike the sherbet mixture** with the cold sake and gelatin mixture. See page 16.

6. **Churn the sherbet** for at least 20 minutes. See page 17.

COOKIES AND CREAM VODKA MILK SHAKE

Cookies and Cream ice cream wasn't around until the early 1980s, and there's great debate as to who invented it. But whoever they are, we tip our vodka-laden scoops to them!

In a blender, combine 2 scoops Cookies and Cream with Vodka ice cream (page 30), ⅓ cup milk, and 2 tablespoons vodka, and blend to combine. Pour into a tall chilled glass and top with 3 crumbled chocolate sandwich cookies.

FIG WITH BARLEY WINE

ICE CREAM   *This ice cream can be an acquired taste. When choosing a barley wine, it's best to get one that's not too hoppy, as the bitterness can pair awkwardly with the dairy. However, there is something kind of tasty about this combination, and we couldn't help but give it a try. The figs give a rich, jammy note to the ice cream while the barley wine adds a wonderful complexity. Please note that soaking the figs takes at least 48 hours, so plan accordingly.*

8 ounces dried Calimyrna figs, divided

¾ cup plus 4 tablespoons sugar, divided

2¾ cups cold (refrigerated) barley wine

1¼ cups milk

1¼ cups heavy cream

1 vanilla bean

pinch of salt

4 egg yolks

1 packet (1 tablespoon) gelatin

⅓ cup cold water

MAKES ABOUT 1 QUART

1 Soak half the figs in barley wine. Remove the stems from 4 or 5 of the figs and cut each one into 8 to 10 small pieces. Place them in a medium jar. Add 2 tablespoons sugar and enough barley wine to cover (½ to ¾ cup). Cover the jar and refrigerate the figs for at least 48 hours, or up to a week (any longer and the figs start to get too soft and lose their body for the ice cream).

When the soaked figs are drunk enough for your liking...

2. Cook the remaining figs. Remove their stems and cut each fig in half. Place them in a small saucepan over

medium-high heat with 2 tablespoons sugar and 1 cup barley wine. Bring to a boil, then reduce the heat to low, cover the pan, and simmer for 15 minutes. Uncover the pan and simmer until half of the liquid has evaporated, about 5 minutes.

3. Puree the cooked figs in a food processor or blender with half the remaining syrup in the pan. Transfer to a large heatproof bowl and set aside.

4. Scald the milk, cream, and sugar with the vanilla bean and salt, using the remaining ¾ cup sugar. See page 11. While the milk mixture is heating, split the vanilla bean down the center lengthwise and scrape out the seeds. Whisk the seeds into the milk mixture, then add the empty pod to the pan.

5. Steep the milk mixture and vanilla. Once the milk mixture is scalding, remove the pan from the heat and cover it. After about 30 minutes, remove the vanilla bean pod.

6. Reheat the milk mixture back up to scalding.

7. Whisk the egg yolks and temper with one-third of the scalding milk mixture. See page 12.

8. Strain, cover, and chill the custard. Strain the custard into the heatproof bowl with the cooked fig puree and stir well. Refrigerate for at least 8 hours. See page 14.

Once the custard is completely cold...

9. Drain the wine-soaked figs. Allow to drain for about 10 minutes. Discard the wine.

10. Dissolve the gelatin in the cold water. See page 15.

11. Spike the custard with 1 cup cold barley wine and the gelatin mixture. See page 16.

12. Churn the ice cream. Don't strain the custard; pour it directly into the ice cream maker and churn for about 15 minutes. Once the ice cream appears to be just a little too fluffy, add the wine-soaked figs to the mixture and churn again until the ice cream thickens, about 5 minutes. If the figs aren't mixed in enough by the time the ice cream is finished churning, you can remove the paddle and gently fold them in by hand while they're still in the freezer bowl. If you don't want to serve the ice cream immediately, or you want a firmer texture, transfer it to a freezer-proof container and freeze for several hours before serving.

EGGNOG WITH BRANDY AND RUM

ICE CREAM *One of the joys of eggnog is that it seems so innocent, with its egg yolks and spiced cream, and yet it has an almost devilish side of dark rum and brandy. This ice cream is as rich as it is flavorful, and it has enough rum and brandy to keep you happy through the holidays. And as in any good eggnog, freshly grated nutmeg adds a special touch.*

1 cup milk

1¾ cups heavy cream

pinch of salt

6 egg yolks

¾ cup sugar

2 teaspoons vanilla extract

1 teaspoon freshly grated nutmeg

1 packet (1 tablespoon) gelatin

⅓ cup cold water

⅓ cup cold (refrigerated) brandy

⅓ cup cold (refrigerated) dark rum

MAKES ABOUT 1 QUART

1 Scald the milk and cream with the salt; don't add the sugar yet. See page 11.

2. Whisk the egg yolks and temper. Whisk the egg yolks with the sugar and temper with one-third of the scalding milk mixture. See page 12.

3. Thicken the custard over low heat. See page 13.

4. Whisk in the vanilla extract and nutmeg.

5. Strain, cover, and chill the custard for at least 8 hours. See page 14.

Once the custard is completely cold...

6. **Dissolve the gelatin** in the cold water. See page 15.

7. **Spike the custard** with the cold brandy, dark rum, and gelatin mixture. See page 16.

8. **Churn the ice cream** for at least 20 minutes. See page 17.

RASPBERRY BELLINI FLOAT

This classic pairing of fresh fruit and chilled sparkling wine would be perfectly refreshing at Mother's Day brunch or Easter...or just a Tuesday afternoon.

Place 2 scoops Raspberry Bellini Sorbet (page 132) in a champagne flute. Fill the glass with prosecco or other sparkling wine, and float a few raspberries on top.

Variation

MIMOSA FLOAT: Substitute Mimosa Sorbet (page 134) for the Raspberry Bellini Sorbet. Instead of raspberries, garnish with an orange twist.

PEACH WITH SCHNAPPS

SHERBET   *Peach Schnapps adds a sweet booziness that everyone who has ever sneaked a sip from their parents' liquor cabinet will recognize.*

6 peaches, peeled, pitted, and chopped

⅓ cup water

¾ cup sugar

1½ cups milk

¾ cup sugar

⅓ cup cold peach Schnapps

MAKES ABOUT 1 QUART

1. Cook the peaches. Place the peaches and the water in a medium saucepan. Simmer over medium heat, covered, until the peaches soften, about 10 minutes.

2. Puree the peaches. Off heat, stir in the sugar. Pour the mixture into a food processor or blender and puree until smooth.

3. Whisk in the milk and the cold peach Schnapps.

4. Cover and chill the mixture for at least 4 hours. See page 14.

Once the mixture is completely cold...

5. Churn the sherbet for at least 20 minutes. See page 17.

RUM RAISIN

ICE CREAM   *This ice cream is rich, and raisins complement rum in every way.*

1 cup raisins

1 cup cold (refrigerated) dark rum, divided, plus more for soaking the raisins

½ cup cold water, divided

1 cup brown sugar

⅛ teaspoon salt

1½ cups milk

1 vanilla bean

4 egg yolks

1 cup heavy cream

½ packet (½ tablespoon) gelatin

MAKES ABOUT 1 QUART

1 **Soak the raisins in rum.** In a medium jar, place the raisins and one-half of the vanilla bean. Add enough rum to cover the raisins. Cover and mix well. Refrigerate for at least 48 hours.

2. **Make the rum syrup.** Mix ½ cup rum, ¼ cup water, and the brown sugar and salt in a small saucepan. Bring to a boil over medium heat and simmer until it's reduced to about half, about 15 minutes. Set aside.

3. **Scald the milk with the remaining one-half vanilla bean.** See page 11. While the milk mixture is heating, split the vanilla bean down the center lengthwise and scrape out the seeds. Whisk the seeds into the milk mixture, then add the empty pod to the pan.

4. **Steep the milk mixture and vanilla.** Once the milk mixture is scalding, remove the pan from the heat and cover it. After about 30 minutes, remove the vanilla bean pod and set it aside.

5. Reheat the milk mixture back up to scalding.

6. Whisk the egg yolks and temper with one-third of the scalding milk mixture. See page 12.

8. Whisk in the rum syrup.

9. Thicken the custard over low heat (see page 13), then strain it into a medium heatproof bowl.

10. Whip the heavy cream. In a large bowl, whisk the heavy cream until it reaches soft peaks. Gently fold the hot custard into the whipped heavy cream.

11. Cover and chill the custard for at least 8 hours. See page 14.

Once the custard is completely cold...

12. Drain the rum raisins. Discard the vanilla bean. Allow to drain for at least 10 minutes.

13. Dissolve the gelatin in the remaining ¼ cup cold water. See page 15.

14. Spike the custard with the remaining ½ cup cold dark rum and gelatin mixture. See page 16.

15. Churn the ice cream for at least 15 minutes. When the ice cream looks fairly fluffy, add the drained rum raisins and churn for another 5 minutes.

GINGER WITH DARK RUM

ICE CREAM   *Fresh ginger gives this ice cream a fierce bite, but the mellowness of brown sugar and the richness of the heavy cream balance out this Dark and Stormy cocktail-inspired treat.*

2 ounces (about 3 inches) fresh ginger, unpeeled

1½ cups milk

1½ cups heavy cream

¾ cup brown sugar

pinch of salt

4 egg yolks

2 teaspoons molasses

½ packet (½ tablespoon) gelatin

⅓ cup cold water

cold juice of 1 lime

½ cup cold (refrigerated) dark rum

MAKES ABOUT 1 QUART

1 **Blanch the ginger.** Bring a small saucepan of water to a boil over high heat. Slice the ginger into nickel-thin rounds. Blanch the ginger slices in the boiling water for 2 minutes, then remove them from the water and set aside.

2. **Scald the milk, cream, and brown sugar** with the salt. See page 11.

3. **Steep the milk mixture and ginger.** Once the milk mixture is scalding, add the blanched ginger, then remove the pan from the heat and cover it. After about 1 hour, strain out the ginger and discard.

4. **Return the milk mixture** back up to scalding.

5. **Whisk the egg yolks and temper** with one-third of the scalding milk mixture. See page 12.

6. **Thicken the custard** over low heat. See page 13.

7. **Whisk in the molasses.**

8. **Strain, cover, and chill the custard** for at least 8 hours. See page 14.

Once the custard is completely cold...

9. **Dissolve the gelatin** in the cold water. See page 15.

10. **Spike the custard** with the cold lime juice, dark rum, and gelatin mixture. See page 16.

11. **Churn the ice cream** for at least 20 minutes. See page 17.

PINK PEPPERCORN WITH VODKA

ICE CREAM   *Pink peppercorns add a soft fruit flavor in addition to their natural sting. Top with Pink Peppercorn Strawberry Compote and the ice cream becomes out of this world. This creation is not for the unadventurous.*

1½ cups milk

1½ cups heavy cream

¾ cup sugar

1 vanilla bean

2 tablespoons whole pink peppercorns

4 egg yolks

2 teaspoons vanilla extract

½ packet (½ tablespoon) gelatin

⅓ cup cold water

½ cup cold (refrigerated) vodka

Pink Peppercorn Strawberry Compote, for serving (recipe follows)

MAKES ABOUT 1 QUART

1. Scald the milk, cream, and sugar with the vanilla bean. See page 11. While the milk mixture is heating, split the vanilla bean down the center lengthwise and scrape out the seeds. Whisk the seeds into the milk mixture, then add the empty pod to the pan along with the pink peppercorns.

2. **Steep the milk mixture, vanilla, and peppercorns.** Once the milk mixture is scalding, remove the pan from the heat and cover it. After about 15 minutes, remove the vanilla bean pod and set it aside. Strain out the peppercorns.

3. **Reheat the milk mixture** back up to scalding.

4. **Whisk the egg yolks and temper** with one-third of the scalding milk mixture. See page 12.

5. **Thicken the custard** over low heat. See page 13.

6. **Whisk in the vanilla extract.**

7. **Strain, cover, and chill the custard** for at least 8 hours. See page 14. Add the empty vanilla bean pod to the custard before covering it.

Once the custard is completely cold...

8. **Remove the vanilla bean pod** from the custard.

9. **Dissolve the gelatin** in the cold water. See page 15.

10. **Spike the ice cream** with the cold vodka and gelatin mixture. See page 1

11. **Churn the ice cream** for at least 20 minutes. See page 17.

12. **Serve** with Pink Peppercorn Strawberry Compote.

PINK PEPPERCORN STRAWBERRY COMPOTE

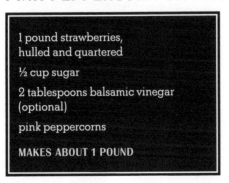

1 pound strawberries, hulled and quartered

½ cup sugar

2 tablespoons balsamic vinegar (optional)

pink peppercorns

MAKES ABOUT 1 POUND

1. Marinate the strawberries. Combine the strawberries, sugar, balsamic vinegar if using, and a few grinds of pink peppercorns in a container with a lid and refrigerate for about 24 hours.

2. When ready to serve, pour the compote into a medium saucepan and stir over medium heat until thick.

COCKTAILS ON A CONE

WHISKEY SHOT

ICE CREAM   *This ice cream is not messing around—you taste whiskey and only a dash of sugar. The milk and heavy cream are used almost just as stabilizers. And it's not just the flavor you'll notice; you'll feel tipsy after just a few spoonfuls. You might want to consider serving your Whiskey Shot in shot glasses.*

You'll need 3 whole cups of whiskey for this recipe. In order not to make it exorbitantly expensive, we used cheap whiskey and it came out perfect. But you can use better quality whiskey if you'd like.

2 cups whiskey plus 1 cup cold whiskey, divided

¼ cup sugar

1 vanilla bean (optional)

1½ cups milk

2 cups heavy cream

4 egg yolks

1 tablespoon cornstarch

1 packet (1 tablespoon) gelatin

¼ cup cold water

MAKES ABOUT 1 QUART

1. Reduce the whiskey. Combine 2 cups whiskey and the sugar in a small saucepan. Split the vanilla bean, if using, down the center lengthwise and scrape out the seeds. Add the seeds and pod to the pan. Simmer over low heat, uncovered, until reduced to about ½ cup, about 5 minutes. Remove the vanilla bean pod and set aside the whiskey syrup.

2. Scald the milk and cream; don't add any sugar. See page 11.

3. Whisk the egg yolks and temper. Whisk the egg yolks with the cornstarch and temper with one-third of the scalding milk mixture. See page 12.

4. Thicken the custard over low heat. See page 13. The custard should thicken rather quickly because of the cornstarch. Whisk in the whiskey syrup.

5. Strain, cover, and chill the custard for at least 8 hours. See page 14.

Once the custard is completely cold...

6. Dissolve the gelatin in the cold water. See page 15.

7. Spike the custard with 1 cup cold whiskey and the gelatin mixture. See page 16.

8. Churn the ice cream for at least 20 minutes. See page 17.

Variations

SCOTCH SHOT: Omit the whiskey. Substitute with Scotch whisky.

BRANDY SHOT: Omit the whiskey. Substitute with brandy.

MANHATTAN

ICE CREAM   *Sophisticated, complex, and decadent—much like the island itself—a Manhattan gets its edgy flavor with the help of rye whiskey. Garnish a scoop with a maraschino cherry and let the creaminess overwhelm you.*

2 cups sweet vermouth

1½ cups milk

1½ cups heavy cream

¾ cup sugar

2 teaspoons bitters

4 egg yolks

½ packet (½ tablespoon) gelatin

⅓ cup cold water

½ cup cold (refrigerated) rye whiskey

maraschino cherries, for garnish

MAKES ABOUT 1 QUART

1. Reduce the vermouth. In a small saucepan, simmer the vermouth over medium heat, uncovered, until reduced to about ½ cup, about 20 minutes. Set aside.

2. Scald the milk, cream, and sugar with the bitters. See page 11.

3. Whisk the egg yolks and temper with one-third of the scalding milk mixture. See page 12.

4. Thicken the custard over low heat. See page 13.

5. Whisk in the reduced sweet vermouth.

6. Strain, cover, and chill the custard for at least 8 hours. See page 14.

Once the custard is completely cold...

7. **Dissolve the gelatin** in the cold water. See page 15.

8. **Spike the custard** with the cold whiskey and gelatin mixture. See page 16.

9. **Churn the ice cream** for at least 20 minutes. See page 17.

10. **Garnish** each serving with a maraschino cherry on top.

IRISH COFFEE AFFOGATO

Affogato *comes from the Italian* affogare, *meaning "to drown." Appropriate, since this treat deliciously pairs cold ice cream drowned in hot coffee, all swimming in a healthy dose of warming Irish whiskey.*

Place 1 scoop Irish Coffee ice cream (page 86) and 1 scoop Whiskey Shot ice cream (page 74) in a coffee mug. Pour a 1-ounce shot of hot coffee or espresso over the top and serve immediately. For an extra kick, add an extra half-shot of whiskey when you add the espresso.

CHOCOLATE MARTINI

ICE CREAM   *There was a time when a martini was a specific kind of cocktail, but today almost any drink can be called a martini if it's served in a martini glass. Luckily for us, this means there's now a chocolate cocktail, which with a few culinary tricks becomes an intoxicatingly tasty ice cream.*

1½ cups milk

1½ cups heavy cream

½ cup sugar

1 teaspoon vanilla extract

4 egg yolks

6 ounces dark chocolate, chopped, or dark chocolate chips

½ packet (½ tablespoon) gelatin

⅓ cup cold water

¼ cup cold (refrigerated) chocolate liqueur

¼ cup cold (refrigerated) vodka or vanilla vodka

MAKES ABOUT 1 QUART

1 Scald the milk, cream, and sugar and the vanilla extract. See page 11.

2. Whisk the egg yolks and temper with one-third of the scalding milk mixture. See page 12.

3. Thicken the custard over low heat. See page 13.

4. Melt the chocolate. Place the chocolate in a large heatproof bowl with a fine-mesh strainer on top. Pour the hot custard through the strainer into the chocolate. Stir until the chocolate is completely melted.

5. Cover, and chill the custard for at least 8 hours. See page 14.

Once the custard is completely cold...

6. Dissolve the gelatin in the cold water. See page 15.

7. Spike the custard with the cold chocolate liqueur, vodka, and gelatin mixture. See page 16.

8. Churn the ice cream for at least 20 minutes. See page 17.

WHISKEY CHOCOLATE MALT

It's like sitting at an old-fashioned soda fountain, except they also serve whiskey.

In a blender, combine ¼ cup milk, 2 tablespoons whiskey, 1¼ cups Chocolate with Irish Whiskey ice cream (page 23), 1½ tablespoons malted-milk powder, and 2 tablespoons Whiskey Chocolate Sauce (page 141). Blend on high just until pureed; do not overmix. Serve in a chilled glass and garnish with chocolate shavings.

Variation

WHISKEY MALT SHOTS: Prepare the whiskey chocolate malt, but instead of serving it in a single tall glass, pour it into several shot glasses. Top each one with a dollop of Boozy Whipped Cream made with whiskey (page 133), and garnish with chocolate shavings. Cheers!

GUINNESS

ICE CREAM   *When it comes to chocolate for this recipe, we think the darker the better. Somehow the bitterness of the chocolate pairs excellently with the almost smokiness of Guinness. This rich ice cream can stand alone, but it's also an essential part of an Irish Shot in an Irish Beer Sundae (page 150).*

¼ cup milk

1 cup heavy cream

½ cup sugar

1 teaspoon vanilla extract

pinch of salt

4 egg yolks

7 ounces dark chocolate, chopped, or dark chocolate chips

1 (12-ounce) cold bottle Guinness, divided

1 packet (1 tablespoon) gelatin

MAKES ABOUT 1 QUART

1. Scald the milk, cream, and sugar with the vanilla extract and salt. See page 11.

2. Whisk the egg yolks and temper with one-third of the scalding milk mixture. See page 12.

3. Thicken the custard over low heat. See page 13.

4. Melt the chocolate. Place the chocolate in a large heatproof bowl with a fine-mesh strainer on top. Pour the hot custard through the strainer into the chocolate. Stir until the chocolate is completely melted.

5. **Cover and chill the custard** for at least 8 hours. See page 14. Pour the custard directly into the container. Don't strain it.

Once the custard is completely cold...

6. **Stir the custard to liquefy** if necessary. Depending on the temperature of your refrigerator, there is a possibility that the custard will have solidified. If that's the case, just blend it as quickly as possible with an immersion blender or a stand blender until it becomes liquid, then continue with the recipe.

7. **Dissolve the gelatin** in ⅓ cup cold Guinness. See page 15.

8. **Spike the custard** with the remaining cold Guinness and the gelatin mixture. See page 16.

9. **Churn the ice cream** for at least 20 minutes. See page 17.

IRISH CREAM

ICE CREAM   *We purposely made this a rich vanilla that's heavy on the egg yolks to pair with the sweet Bailey's Irish Cream. We were also pleasantly surprised that the extra egg yolks allowed the ice cream to solidify without our usual helper, gelatin.*

1½ cups milk

1¼ cups heavy cream

1 vanilla bean

pinch of salt

6 egg yolks

½ cup sugar

¾ cup cold (refrigerated) Bailey's Irish Cream

MAKES ABOUT 1 QUART

1. **Scald the milk and cream** with the vanilla bean and salt; don't add the sugar yet. See page 11. While the milk mixture is heating, split the vanilla bean down the center lengthwise and scrape out the seeds. Whisk the seeds into the milk mixture, then add the empty pod to the pan.

2. **Steep the milk mixture and vanilla.** Once the milk mixture is scalding, remove the pan from the heat and cover it. After about 30 minutes, remove the vanilla bean pod and set it aside.

3. **Reheat the milk mixture** back up to scalding.

4. **Whisk the egg yolks and temper.** Whisk the egg yolks with the sugar in a medium bowl until they're light in color and slightly fluffy and temper with one-third of the scalding milk mixture. See page 12.

5. **Thicken the custard** over low heat. See page 13.

6. **Strain, cover, and chill the custard** for at least 8 hours. See page 14. Add the empty vanilla bean pod to the custard before covering it.

Once the custard is completely cold...

7. **Remove the vanilla bean pod** from the custard.

8. **Whisk the cold Bailey's Irish Cream** into the custard until combined.

9. **Churn the ice cream** for at least 20 minutes. See page 17.

IRISH COFFEE

ICE CREAM   *For years, many people have taken comfort in Irish coffee after a long night out. Instead of heating whole coffee beans in milk like in Coffee with Kahlúa (page 34), we use cold brewing. This procedure draws out the true flavor of coffee without altering it with the heat of hot water, so you taste coffee without the bitterness. And when this ice cream is topped with Irish Coffee Whipped Ice Cream, you can't beat the combination. Warning: Cold brewing takes at least 48 hours. Plan accordingly.*

¾ cup milk

1½ cups heavy cream

¾ cup sugar

4 egg yolks

¾ cup Cold-Brew Milk Coffee (recipe follows)

1 packet (1 tablespoon) gelatin

⅓ cup cold water

⅔ cup cold (refrigerated) Irish whiskey

Irish Cream Whipped Ice Cream (page 93), to serve

MAKES ABOUT 1 QUART

1 Scald the milk, cream, and sugar. See page 11.

2. Whisk the egg yolks and temper with one-third of the scalded milk mixture. See page 12.

3. Thicken the custard over low heat. See page 13.

4. Whisk in the cold-brew milk coffee.

5. Strain, cover, and chill the custard for at least 8 hours. See page 14.

Once the custard is completely cold...

6. Dissolve the gelatin in the cold water. See page 15.

7. Spike the custard with the cold Irish whiskey and gelatin mixture. See page 16.

8. Churn the ice cream for at least 20 minutes. See page 17.

9. Serve with Irish Cream Whipped Ice Cream on top.

COLD-BREW MILK COFFEE

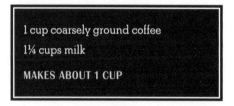

1 cup coarsely ground coffee

1¼ cups milk

MAKES ABOUT 1 CUP

1. Steep the coffee grounds. Mix the coffee grounds and milk in a jar and cover. Allow to steep, covered, in the refrigerator for at least 48 hours and up to a week. Stir occasionally.

2. Strain the coffee grounds. When you're ready to use the coffee, strain out the coffee grounds; it's okay if some of the finer pieces of coffee get through.

WHITE RUSSIAN

ICE CREAM   *Of all the ice cream suggestions we gathered for this book, this was probably the most requested flavor—Kahlúa and vodka mixed with rich heavy cream. We like to think The Dude would enjoy eating a bowl of this ice cream on his new rug.*

½ cup milk

2½ cups heavy cream

½ cup sugar

4 egg yolks

1 packet (1 tablespoon) gelatin

¼ cup cold water

⅔ cup cold (refrigerated) vodka

⅔ cup cold (refrigerated) Kahlúa

MAKES ABOUT 1 QUART

1. Scald the milk, cream, and sugar. See page 11.

2. Whisk the egg yolks and temper with one-third of the scalding milk mixture. See page 12.

3. Thicken the custard over low heat. See page 13.

4. Strain, cover, and chill the custard for at least 8 hours. See page 14.

Once the custard is completely cold...

5. Dissolve the gelatin in the cold water. See page 15.

6. Spike the custard with the cold vodka, Kahlúa, and gelatin mixture. See page 16.

7. Churn the ice cream for at least 20 minutes. See page 17.

WHISKEY COLA

ICE CREAM   *You see it at almost every party: bottles of liquor next to bottles of cola. Sometimes it's generic, sometimes it's name brand. It doesn't matter. Cola pairs strangely well with strong booze. This recipe uses whiskey, but you can, of course, switch it up and use another strong liquor of your choosing.*

2 cups cola plus ¼ cup cold cola, divided

3 allspice berries

1 whole clove

1½ cups milk

1½ cups heavy cream

4 egg yolks

¾ cup sugar

½ packet (½ tablespoon) gelatin

½ cup cold (refrigerated) whiskey

MAKES ABOUT 1 QUART

1 **Reduce the cola.** In a small saucepan, heat 2 cups cola and the allspice berries and clove over low heat. Simmer, uncovered, until reduced by half, about 10 minutes. Strain out the allspice berries and clove and discard. Set aside the cola syrup and allow to cool.

2. **Scald the milk and cream,** but don't add the sugar yet. See page 11.

3. **Whisk the egg yolks and temper.** Whisk the egg yolks with the sugar and temper with one-third of the scalding milk mixture. See page 12.

4. **Thicken the custard** over low heat. See page 13.

5. **Whisk in the reduced cola.**

6. **Strain, cover, and chill the custard** for at least 8 hours. See page 14.

Once the custard is completely cold...

7. **Dissolve the gelatin** in the ¼ cup cold cola. See page 15.

8. **Spike the custard** with the cold whiskey and gelatin mixture. See page 16.

9. **Churn the ice cream** for at least 20 minutes. See page 17.

Variation

RUM AND COLA: Omit the whiskey. Substitute with rum.

WHISKEY SOUR

SHERBET   *This sherbert combines a fresh lemon taste with the warm, woody flavor of whiskey. Lower-quality whiskey will work well in this recipe, but if it's a special occasion, it's worth going for top-shelf.*

1½ cups milk, divided

¾ cup sugar

grated zest of 1 lemon

1½ cups heavy cream

½ cup cold fresh lemon juice (from 4 to 6 lemons)

1 packet (1 tablespoon) gelatin

⅓ cup cold water

¾ cup cold (refrigerated) blended whiskey

MAKES ABOUT 1 QUART

1 Make the syrup. In a medium saucepan, combine 1 cup milk and the sugar and lemon zest and simmer over low heat until the sugar is completely dissolved, about 5 minutes.

2. Whisk in the heavy cream and the remaining ½ cup milk.

3. Cover and chill the mixture for at least 4 hours. See page 14.

Once the mixture is completely cold...

4. Whisk the lemon juice into the sherbet mixture. If you see curdling, immediately whisk until smooth.

5. Dissolve the gelatin in the cold water. See page 15.

6. **Spike the sherbet mixture** with the cold blended whiskey and gelatin mixture. See page 16.

7. **Churn the sherbet** for at least 20 minutes. See page 17.

IRISH CREAM WHIPPED ICE CREAM

MAKES ABOUT 2 CUPS

Unlike our other Irish Cream ice cream (page 84), this one does not require an ice cream maker. It's super easy to make and unbelievably light, sweet, and silky.

Combine 1 cup heavy cream, ¼ cup Irish cream, and ¾ cup confectioners' sugar in a medium bowl. Whisk gently until the sugar dissolves. Then whisk a little more vigorously until the cream begins to thicken and hold a shape, yet remains smooth. (You want to avoid whipping it to stiff peaks.) Transfer the whipped cream to a freezer-proof container and freeze for at least 4 hours. Scoop out like regular ice cream!

COSMOPOLITAN

ICE CREAM   *Thanks to a little TV show about single women living in New York City, Cosmopolitans have become ingrained in our nation's psyche as the cocktail to enjoy with one's girlfriends. This ice cream will remind you why the drink became so popular in the first place (it's delicious!).*

8 ounces fresh or frozen cranberries

⅔ cup cold water, divided

1 cup sugar, divided

1 cup milk

1 cup heavy cream

2 egg yolks

¼ cup Rose's Lime Juice or fresh lime juice

½ packet (½ tablespoon) gelatin

½ cup cold (refrigerated) vodka

¼ cup cold (refrigerated) triple sec

MAKES ABOUT 1 QUART

1 **Cook the cranberries.** Combine the cranberries, ⅓ cup cold water, and ¼ cup sugar in a large saucepan and bring to a boil over high heat, stirring periodically to prevent sticking, then reduce the heat to medium and simmer until most of the skins have popped and the cranberries resemble preserves, about 15 minutes.

2. **Puree the cranberries.** Once the cranberries are cooked, immediately puree them in a food processor or blender. Note: Do not allow to cool first because the cranberry mixture may start to gel due to the release of pectin from cooking. Carefully strain the hot cranberry mixture into a large heatproof bowl and set aside.

3. Scald the milk, cream, and sugar using the remaining ¾ cup sugar. See page 11.

4. Whisk the egg yolks and temper with one-third of the scalding milk mixture. See page 12.

5. Thicken the custard over low heat. See page 13.

6. Strain, cover, and chill the custard. Strain the custard into the cranberry mixture, add the Rose's Lime Juice or fresh lime juice, and whisk until combined. Refrigerate for at least 8 hours. See page 14.

Once the custard is completely cold...

7. Dissolve the gelatin in the remaining ⅓ cup cold water. See page 15.

8. Spike the custard with the cold vodka, triple sec, and gelatin mixture. See page 16.

9. Churn the ice cream for at least 20 minutes. See page 17. Don't strain the custard; pour it directly into the ice cream maker.

TROPICAL TREATS BY THE SCOOP

STRAWBERRY DAIQUIRI

ICE CREAM *No matter where you go in the world, you can probably find yourself a strawberry daiquiri. This scoopable daiquiri will surely bring delight to all those who partake in its sweetness.*

2 pounds strawberries, hulled and quartered

1 cup sugar, divided

¼ cup water

2 ounces triple sec, divided

1¾ cups milk

1¼ cups heavy cream

4 egg yolks

1 packet (1 tablespoon) gelatin

¾ cup cold (refrigerated) white rum

MAKES ABOUT 1 QUART

1 Cook the strawberries. In a large saucepan, combine the strawberries, ¼ cup sugar, and the water and simmer over medium heat until the strawberries have softened, 15 to 20 minutes.

2. Puree the hot strawberries immediately in a food processor or blender. Strain the puree through a fine-mesh strainer into a large heatproof bowl. Whisk in 1 ounce triple sec. Measure 2 cups puree into a medium bowl and 3 ounces puree (roughly 3 shot glasses worth) into a small saucepan or microwave-safe container. Set aside.

3. Scald the milk and cream; don't add the sugar yet. See page 11.

4. Whisk the egg yolks and temper. Whisk the egg yolks with the remaining ¾ cup sugar in a medium bowl until lighter in color and slightly fluffy and temper with one-third of the scalding milk mixture. See page 12.

5. Thicken the custard over low heat. See page 13.

6. Strain, cover, and chill the custard. Strain the custard into the 2 cups strawberry puree and whisk until combined and refrigerate for at least 8 hours. See page 14.

Once the custard is completely cold...

8. Dissolve the gelatin in the 3 ounces strawberry puree. See page 15.

9. Spike the custard with the cold white rum, remaining 1 ounce triple sec, and gelatin mixture. See page 16.

10. Churn the ice cream for at least 20 minutes. See page 17.

MARGARITA

SORBET   *Fresh lime juice is key for this sorbet's flavor. Don't use concentrate and don't even think about using the plastic lime-shaped squeeze bottles.*

2½ cups cold water, divided

½ cup sugar

grated zest of 3 limes

1½ cups cold fresh lime juice

½ packet (½ tablespoon) gelatin

1½ ounces cold (refrigerated) Cointreau

2½ ounces cold (refrigerated) white tequila

MAKES ABOUT 1 QUART

1 **Make the syrup.** In a medium saucepan, combine 2 cups water and the sugar and lime zest and simmer over medium heat until the sugar is completely dissolved, about 5 minutes. Remove the pan from the heat, cover it, and steep for at least 15 minutes.

2. **Cover and chill the syrup** for at least 4 hours.

Once the syrup is completely cold...

3. **Add the juice.** Pour the cold lime juice into a large bowl. Stream the cold syrup into the juice and whisk until combined.

4. **Dissolve the gelatin** in the remaining ½ cup cold water. See page 15.

5. **Spike the syrup** with the cold Cointreau, tequila, and gelatin mixture. See page 16.

6. **Churn the sorbet** for at least 20 minutes. See page 17.

MANGO MARGARITA

ICE CREAM   *This ice cream has a velvety texture and is chock-full of mango flavor. Rose's Lime Juice, a classic cocktail ingredient popular with bartenders and available at most supermarkets, adds a well-balanced zest that we didn't get with fresh lime juice, but use what you can find.*

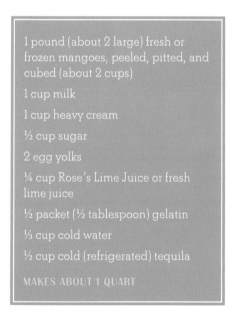

1 pound (about 2 large) fresh or frozen mangoes, peeled, pitted, and cubed (about 2 cups)

1 cup milk

1 cup heavy cream

½ cup sugar

2 egg yolks

¼ cup Rose's Lime Juice or fresh lime juice

½ packet (½ tablespoon) gelatin

⅓ cup cold water

½ cup cold (refrigerated) tequila

MAKES ABOUT 1 QUART

1. **Puree the mango** in a blender or food processor until smooth.

2. **Reduce the mango puree** in a small saucepan. Simmer over low heat, stirring frequently to prevent sticking, until it reaches an almost jam-like consistency, about 45 minutes. Pour into a large heatproof bowl and set aside. *Note:* You might notice that the color of the mango darkens a bit. That's okay. You won't notice it in the end.

3. **Scald the milk, cream, and sugar.** See page 11.

4. **Whisk the egg yolks and temper** with one-third of the scalding milk mixture. See page 12.

5. Strain, cover, and chill the custard. Strain the custard into the mango puree and add the Rose's Lime Juice or fresh lime juice. Whisk until combined. Refrigerate for at least 8 hours. See page 14.

Once the custard is completely cold...

6. Dissolve the gelatin in the cold water. See page 15.

7. Spike the custard with the cold tequila and gelatin mixture. See page 16.

8. Churn the ice cream for at least 20 minutes. See page 17. Don't strain the custard; pour it directly into the ice cream maker.

Variations

PEACH MARGARITA: Omit the mangoes. Substitute with 1 pound of peaches.

NO GELATIN: The amount of trial and error it took to make this flavor was kind of astounding. One batch came out too custardy. Another had so much tequila you couldn't taste the mango. Finding the right balance was extremely difficult, but it was well worth it. We found that just ¼ cup tequila had a good amount of flavor, and using less alcohol means you don't need the gelatin as a stabilizer. To make this ice cream without gelatin, omit the gelatin and water. Reduce the tequila to ¼ cup and whisk it directly into the cold custard before you churn the ice cream.

POMEGRANATE MARGARITA

ICE CREAM   *Getting your daily dose of antioxidants is a little more fun with this brightly colored ice cream. Pomegranate juice might be a bit hard to find; if you can't track it down, we've included instructions for quickly making your own puree. If you manage to make more than 1 cup puree, you can freeze the rest for later use.*

1 cup pomegranate juice, or 3 large or 4 small pomegranates

1½ cups milk

1 cup heavy cream

½ cup sugar, divided

4 egg yolks

½ packet (½ tablespoon) gelatin

⅓ cup cold water

¼ cup cold (refrigerated) tequila

¼ cup cold (refrigerated) triple sec

¼ cup cold fresh lime juice

MAKES ABOUT 1 QUART

If using pomegranate juice, proceed to step 3.

1. Puree the pomegranate seeds. Remove the seeds from the pomegranates and puree them in a food processor or blender.

2. Heat the pomegranate seeds in a small saucepan over low heat until the puree loosens up just a little bit. Do not let it bubble. Strain the puree through a fine-mesh strainer into a medium heatproof bowl and set aside. Note: You'll have to strain the seeds slowly and in stages due to all the seed fragments you're straining out. You can speed up the process by using a flat-bottomed surface, such as the bottom of a glass, to push down on the pulp and extract the juice.

3. Scald the milk, cream, and sugar using ¼ cup sugar. See page 11.

4. Whisk the egg yolks and temper. Whisk the egg yolks with the remaining ¼ cup sugar until lighter in color and slightly fluffy and temper with one-third of the scalding milk mixture. See page 12.

5. Thicken the custard over low heat. See page 13.

6. Whisk in the pomegranate juice.

7. Strain, cover, and chill the custard for at least 8 hours. See page 14. If you used fresh pomegranates and made your own juice, the custard may strain slowly.

Once the custard is completely cold...

8. Dissolve the gelatin in the cold water. See page 15.

9. Spike the custard with the cold tequila, triple sec, and gelatin mixture. See page 16.

10. Whisk in the cold lime juice.

11. Churn the ice cream for at least 20 minutes. See page 17. Don't strain the custard; pour it directly into the ice cream maker.

BLUE HAWAIIAN ICE CREAM

ICE CREAM *For reasons still unknown, we became obsessed with the idea of blue ice cream. Luckily, the Blue Hawaiian cocktail made with pineapple and coconut cream gained a heavy dose of color with the help of blue curaçao.*

½ pineapple, peeled, cored, and diced

½ cup plus 2 tablespoons sugar, divided

1¼ cups milk

1 (15-ounce) can coconut cream

4 egg yolks

1 packet (1 tablespoon) gelatin

⅓ cup cold water

⅔ cup cold (refrigerated) white rum

⅔ cup cold (refrigerated) blue curaçao

Garnishes

pineapple slices

whipped cream

maraschino cherries

MAKES ABOUT 1 QUART

1 **Puree the pineapple** in a food processor or blender to yield about 1¾ cups puree.

2. **Reduce the pineapple puree.** Combine the pineapple puree and 2 tablespoons sugar in a medium saucepan. Simmer on low heat until reduced to about half, about 30 minutes. Cover, set aside to cool, then refrigerate until cold.

3. **Scald the milk, coconut cream, and sugar** using the remaining ½ cup sugar. See page 11.

4. **Whisk the egg yolks and temper** with one-third of the scalding milk mixture. See page 12.

5. Thicken the custard over low heat. See page 13.

6. Strain, cover, and chill the custard for at least 8 hours. See page 14.

Once the custard is completely cold...

7. Pour the cold custard into a large bowl and fold in the cold pineapple puree.

8. Dissolve the gelatin in the cold water. See page 15.

9. Spike the custard with the cold rum, blue curaçao, and gelatin mixture. See page 16.

10. Churn the ice cream for at least 15 minutes. See page 17. Don't strain the custard; pour it directly into the ice cream maker. Be careful not to overchurn this ice cream, or it will get a flaky texture.

11. Garnish each serving with a pineapple slice, whipped cream, and a maraschino cherry on top.

PIÑA COLADA

ICE CREAM   *Buttermilk lends an extra tang to this ice cream. Whole chunks of pineapple covered in simple syrup and toasted coconut give a multidimensional take on the classic cocktail.*

1 cup unsweetened shredded coconut

2 cups sugar, divided

½ cup water

2 cups buttermilk

1 cup heavy cream

1¾ pound fresh pineapple, cut into bite-size chunks

4 egg yolks

1 cup cold (refrigerated) white rum, divided

1 packet (1 tablespoon) gelatin

MAKES ABOUT 1 QUART

1 **Toast the coconut.** Preheat the oven to 350°F. Spread the shredded coconut on a cookie sheet and bake until golden brown, about 3 minutes. It's fine if some slightly untoasted white shreds of coconut are left. Set aside.

2. **Make the simple syrup.** In a small saucepan, combine 1 cup sugar and the water and simmer over medium-low heat until the sugar dissolves, about 5 minutes. You should have at least 1½ cups. Set aside.

3. **Scald the buttermilk and heavy cream;** don't add any sugar yet. See page 11.

4. Steep the buttermilk mixture and coconut. Once the buttermilk is scalding, remove the pan from the heat, add the toasted coconut, and cover the pan. After 10 minutes, strain out the coconut and discard.

5. Puree the pineapple. While the coconut steeps, in a blender or food processor, puree ¾ pound pineapple with about ¾ cup simple syrup. Strain the puree into a large heatproof bowl. Reserve about ¼ cup puree in a separate container and refrigerate.

6. Return the buttermilk mixture back up to scalding.

7. Whisk the egg and temper. Whisk the egg yolks with the remaining 1 cup sugar and temper with one-third of the scalding buttermilk mixture. See page 12.

8. Thicken the custard over low heat. See page 13.

9. Strain, cover, and chill the custard. Strain the custard into the pineapple puree in the large bowl and whisk until combined. Refrigerate for at least 8 hours. See page 14.

10. Soak the pineapple in simple syrup. Mix ¼ cup white rum into the remaining ¾ cup simple syrup. In a separate container, cover 1 pound pineapple with the simple syrup and rum mixture. Cover and refrigerate until cold.

Once the custard is completely cold...

11. Dissolve the gelatin in the reserved cold pineapple puree. See page 15.

12. Spike the custard with the remaining ¾ cup cold white rum and the gelatin mixture.

13. Churn the custard for at least 20 minutes. See page 17. If you don't want to serve the ice cream immediately, don't put it in the freezer yet.

14. Add the syrup-soaked pineapple. Scoop about one-quarter of the ice cream into a freezer-proof container and add about one-quarter of the syrup-soaked pineapple on top. Repeat the layers three more times with the remaining ice cream and pineapple. Freeze until ready to serve.

RUM PINEAPPLE TOPPING

MAKES ABOUT 2 CUPS

In a medium saucepan over medium high heat, combine 1 pound pineapple cut into bite-size chunks, 2 tablespoons sugar, and 2 tablespoons rum. Cook, stirring occasionally, until the sauce thickens, about 5 minutes. Remove from the heat. Transfer about one-third of the sauce to a blender or food processor and puree, then return the puree to the saucepan and stir to combine.

TROPICAL BREEZE

ICE CREAM   *Pineapple, bananas, and oranges make an idyllic combination with coconut rum in this ice cream. It's best served while looking out at the ocean in Hawaii, but it'll also be terrific at a luau-themed party. When it comes to pineapple, fresh is best, but canned or frozen will do. Just make sure you drain it thoroughly.*

1 cup milk

½ cup heavy cream

½ cup sugar

1 teaspoon vanilla extract

2 egg yolks

8 ounces cold pineapple chunks

1 medium cold ripe banana

3 tablespoons cold fresh orange juice

1 packet (1 tablespoon) gelatin

⅓ cup cold water

¾ cup cold (refrigerated) coconut rum

¼ cup cold (refrigerated) triple sec

MAKES ABOUT 1 QUART

1. Scald the milk, cream, and sugar and the vanilla extract. See page 11.

2. Whisk the egg yolks and temper with one-third of the scalding milk mixture. See page 12.

3. **Thicken the custard** over low heat. See page 13.

4. **Strain, cover, and chill the custard** for at least 8 hours. See page 14.

Once the custard is completely cold...

5. **Puree the fruit.** In a blender or food processor, puree the cold pineapple, banana, and orange juice until thoroughly blended.

6. **Pour the cold custard into a large bowl** and fold in the cold fruit puree.

7. **Dissolve the gelatin** in the cold water. See page 15.

8. **Spike the custard** with the cold rum, triple sec, and gelatin mixture. See page 16.

9. **Churn the ice cream** for at least 20 minutes. See page 17. Don't strain the custard; pour it directly into the ice cream maker.

DRUNKEN MARASCHINO CHERRIES

MAKES 1 CUP

What sundae would be complete without a cherry on top? A jar of these tipsy toppers is enough for more than one sundae, but your friends probably won't mind when you invite them over to share the wealth.

Place 1 cup maraschino cherries in a medium jar and add enough liquor (like brandy or vodka) to cover. Cover the jar and refrigerate the brandied cherries for 48 hours, or up to a week.

BAHAMA MAMA

ICE CREAM   *Fruit and rum, almost any kind of rum, makes a wonderful combination. The Bahama Mama highlights these flavors' merry marriage.*

1 pineapple, peeled, cored, and cubed

½ cup plus 2 tablespoons sugar, divided

1¼ cups milk

1¼ cups heavy cream

4 egg yolks

1 packet (1 tablespoon) gelatin

⅓ cup cold water

¼ cup cold (refrigerated) dark rum

¼ cup cold (refrigerated) white rum

¼ cup cold (refrigerated) coconut liqueur

2 tablespoons cold (refrigerated) coffee liqueur

cold juice of 1 lemon

MAKES ABOUT 1 QUART

1 **Puree the pineapple** in a blender or food processor to yield about 3 cups puree.

2. **Reduce the pineapple puree.** Combine the pineapple puree and 2 tablespoons sugar in a medium saucepan. Simmer on low heat until reduced to about half, about 30 minutes. Set aside and allow to cool, then refrigerate until cold.

3. **Scald the milk, cream, and sugar** using the remaining ½ cup sugar. See page 11.

4. **Whisk the egg yolks and temper** with one-third of the scalding milk mixture. See page 12.

5. **Thicken the custard** over low heat. See page 13.

6. **Strain, cover, and chill the custard** for at least 8 hours. See page 14.

Once the custard is completely cold...

7. **Pour the cold custard into a large bowl** and fold in the cold pineapple puree.

8. **Dissolve the gelatin** in the cold water. See page 15.

9. **Spike the custard** with the cold dark rum, white rum, coconut liqueur, coffee liqueur, lemon juice, and gelatin mixture. See page 16.

10. **Churn the ice cream** for at least 20 minutes. See page 17. Don't strain the custard; pour it directly into the ice cream maker.

MOJITO

SORBET   *This light and refreshing sorbet gives a satisfying hit of white rum with mint and lime that's perfect for summertime (or whenever you wish it were summertime). For an added flair, garnish with candied mint.*

2½ cups water plus⅓ cup cold water, divided

¾ cup sugar

1 bunch mint (about 1 cup leaves)

grated zest of 2 limes

¾ cup fresh lime juice (from 4 to 6 limes)

½ packet (½ tablespoon) gelatin

½ cup cold (refrigerated) white rum

candied mint, for garnish (recipe follows)

MAKES ABOUT 1 QUART

1 **Make the syrup.** In a medium saucepan, mix 2½ cups water and the sugar until dissolved. Bring to a simmer over low heat.

2. **Prepare the mint leaves.** Set aside 20 mint leaves. While waiting for the syrup mixture to simmer, bruise the remaining mint leaves with either a mortar and pestle or the backside of a kitchen knife.

3. **Steep the syrup.** Once the sugar is dissolved, add the lime zest and the bruised mint leaves to the simmering syrup. Remove the pan from the heat, cover, and steep for 20 minutes.

4. **Strain, cover, and chill the syrup.** Strain the syrup into a medium heatproof bowl and whisk in the lime juice. Chill for at least 4 hours.

Once the syrup is completely cold...

5. Dissolve the gelatin in ⅓ cup cold water. See page 15.

6. Spike the syrup with the cold white rum and gelatin mixture. See page 16.

7. Churn the sorbet. Strain the syrup into the ice cream maker and churn. After about 10 minutes, stack 5 of the reserved mint leaves, going in the same direction, and roll them like a cigar. Slice them evenly with a kitchen knife into fine ribbons. This is called chiffonade. Repeat with the remaining mint leaves, then add them to the sorbet in the ice cream maker and allow the mint to be mixed in.

After about 20 minutes, turn off the ice cream maker and remove the paddle. If the mint doesn't look evenly mixed in, gently fold the leaves into the sorbet until just thoroughly blended. Do not overwork it. If you don't want to serve the sorbet immediately, or you want a firmer texture, transfer it to a freezer-proof container and freeze for several hours before serving.

8. Serve with candied mint, if desired. Put a scoop of sorbet in a glass and slide a candied mint leaf into the side.

CANDIED MINT

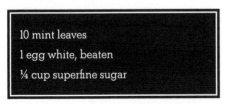

10 mint leaves
1 egg white, beaten
¼ cup superfine sugar

1. Brush the mint leaves gently with the egg white.

2. Sugar the mint leaves. Pour the sugar onto a plate and gently press the mint leaves down into it on both sides. Allow the leaves to dry on parchment paper for 12 hours.

ALABAMA SLAMMER

SHERBET   *We've only visited the South a few times, but we'd like to think that Southerners would enjoy this ice cream filled with amaretto and gin.*

1 cup sugar

2 cups fresh orange juice

1 tablespoon fresh lemon juice

1½ cups milk

1 teaspoon vanilla extract or almond extract

1 packet (1 tablespoon) gelatin

⅓ cup cold water

¼ cup cold (refrigerated) amaretto

¼ cup cold (refrigerated) Southern Comfort

¼ cup cold (refrigerated) sloe gin

MAKES ABOUT 1 QUART

1 **Make the syrup.** Whisk the sugar, orange juice, and lemon juice together until the sugar is completely dissolved.

2. **Whisk in the milk** and vanilla or almond extract.

3. **Cover and chill the syrup** for at least 4 hours. See page 14.

Once the syrup is completely cold...

4. **Dissolve the gelatin** in the cold water. See page 15.

5. **Spike the syrup** with the cold amaretto, Southern Comfort, sloe gin, and gelatin mixture. See page 16.

6. **Churn the sherbet** for at least 20 minutes. See page 17.

HURRICANE

SORBET   *A Hurricane is almost a requirement for wandering around the French Quarter in New Orleans. Sweet and citrusy, the drink goes down easy, and so does this sorbet.*

1 cup water

½ cup sugar

grated zest of ½ orange

grated zest of ½ lime

1 cup passion fruit puree

1 cup fresh orange juice

juice of 1 lime

1 cup cold pineapple juice, divided

½ packet (½ tablespoon) gelatin

2 ounces cold (refrigerated) dark rum

2 ounces cold (refrigerated) light rum

4 dashes bitters

MAKES ABOUT 1 QUART

1 **Make the syrup.** In a medium saucepan, combine the water, sugar, orange zest, and lime zest and simmer over medium heat until the sugar is completely dissolved, about 5 minutes. Remove the pan from the heat, cover it, and steep for at least 15 minutes.

2. **Strain, cover, and chill the syrup** for at least 4 hours.

3. **Chill the juices.** In a large bowl, whisk together the passion fruit puree, orange juice, lime juice, and ½ cup pineapple juice. Refrigerate until cold.

Once the syrup and juice are completely cold...

4. **Whisk the cold syrup** into the bowl with the cold juices.

5. **Dissolve the gelatin** in the remaining ½ cup cold pineapple juice. See page 15.

6. **Spike the syrup** with the cold dark rum, light rum, bitters, and gelatin mixture. See page 16.

7. **Churn the sorbet** for at least 20 minutes. See page 17. Don't strain the syrup; pour it directly into the ice cream maker.

SPIKED SORBETS AND SHERBETS

LEMON DROP

SHERBET   *You're going to want to pucker up to this lemony treat. It's as intoxicating as it is refreshing, and it should appeal to both fruity drink lovers and casual drinkers alike. Please take note: Don't try to combine steps, such as adding the lemon juice before chilling the custard. The acid from the lemon juice will cause the milk to curdle in a not-so-pleasant way.*

1½ cups milk, divided

¾ cup sugar

grated zest of 1 lemon

1½ cups heavy cream

½ cup cold fresh lemon juice (from 4 to 6 lemons)

½ packet (½ tablespoon) gelatin

⅓ cup cold water

½ cup cold (refrigerated) vodka

MAKES ABOUT 1 QUART

1. Make the syrup. In a medium saucepan, stir 1 cup milk and the sugar and lemon zest over low heat until the sugar is completely dissolved, about 5 minutes.

2. Whisk in the heavy cream and the remaining ½ cup milk.

3. Cover and chill the mixture for at least 4 hours. See page 14. Before refrigerating, place the bowl in an ice bath for 30 minutes.

Once the mixture is completely cold...

4. Whisk the cold lemon juice into the cold sherbet mixture. If you see curdling, immediately whisk until smooth.

5. **Dissolve the gelatin** in the cold water. See page 15.

6. **Spike the mixture** with the cold vodka and gelatin mixture. See page 16.

7. **Churn the sherbet** for at least 20 minutes. See page 17.

Variation

SIDECAR: Omit the vodka. Spike with ½ cup brandy and ¼ cup Grand Marnier or Cointreau. Increase the gelatin to 1 full packet (1 tablespoon).

CAPE COD

SHERBET   *The milk in this sherbet cuts the acidity of the cranberries. Fresh and creamy, this flavor is an excellent addition to Sex on the Beach Rainbow Sherbet (page 149).*

12 ounces fresh or frozen cranberries

1⅓ cups water plus 2 tablespoons cold water, divided

1½ cups sugar

2¼ cups milk

1 packet (1 tablespoon) gelatin

¾ cup cold (refrigerated) vodka

MAKES ABOUT 1 QUART

1. **Cook the cranberries.** Combine the cranberries, ⅓ cup water, and the sugar in a large saucepan and bring to a boil over high heat, stirring periodically to prevent sticking, then reduce the heat to low and simmer until most of the skins have popped and the cranberries resemble preserves, about 15 minutes.

2. **Puree the cranberries.** Once the cranberries are cooked, immediately puree them in a food processor or blender. Note: Do not allow to cool first because the cranberry mixture may start to gel due to the release of pectin from cooking.

3. **Strain, cover, and chill the mixture.** Carefully strain the hot cranberry mixture into a large heatproof bowl and whisk in the milk. Chill for at least 4 hours. See page 14. Before refrigerating, place the bowl in an ice bath for 30 minutes.

Once the mixture is completely cold...

4. Dissolve the gelatin in 2 tablespoons cold water. See page 15.

5. Spike the sherbet mixture with the cold vodka and gelatin mixture. See page 16.

6. Churn the mixture for at least 15 minutes. See page 17. Don't strain the mixture; pour it directly into the ice cream maker.

VODKA STRAWBERRY TOPPING

MAKES ABOUT 2 CUPS

Stem, hull, and quarter 2 pints strawberries. In a medium saucepan over medium-high heat, combine the strawberries, 2 tablespoons sugar, and 2 tablespoons vodka. Cook, stirring occasionally, until the sauce thickens, about 5 minutes. Remove from the heat. Transfer about one-third of the sauce to a blender or food processor and puree, then return the puree to the saucepan and stir to combine.

SCREWDRIVER

SHERBET   *There's nothing like elevating a well-known hangover drink into something as sophisticated as a sherbet. As the drinking crowd knows, vodka doesn't have a distinctive flavor. However, it does manage to be an interesting flavor enhancer, and this sherbet is no exception. The orange juice gets a great kick from its deceptively complex alcohol companion.*

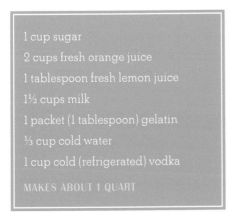

1 cup sugar

2 cups fresh orange juice

1 tablespoon fresh lemon juice

1½ cups milk

1 packet (1 tablespoon) gelatin

⅓ cup cold water

1 cup cold (refrigerated) vodka

MAKES ABOUT 1 QUART

1 **Make the syrup.** Whisk the sugar, orange juice, and lemon juice together until the sugar is completely dissolved.

2. **Whisk in the milk.**

3. **Cover and chill the syrup** for at least 4 hours. See page 14.

Once the syrup is completely cold…

4. **Dissolve the gelatin** in the cold water. See page 15.

5. **Spike the syrup** with the cold vodka and gelatin mixture. See page 16.

6. **Churn the sherbet** for at least 20 minutes. See page 17.

CHAMPAGNE AND STRAWBERRIES

SORBET   *The classic combination of strawberries and champagne gets a kick from balsamic vinegar and fresh black pepper. The pepper is optional, but we highly recommend it because it brings out a different dimension in the strawberries.*

1 pound strawberries, hulled and quartered (about 3 cups)

3 tablespoons balsamic vinegar

½ cup water plus ⅓ cup cold water, divided

½ cup sugar

grated zest of 2 lemons

2 tablespoons fresh lemon juice

1 packet (1 tablespoon) gelatin

1½ cups cold (refrigerated) champagne

freshly cracked black pepper, to serve (optional)

MAKES ABOUT 1 QUART

1 Marinate the strawberries. In a medium bowl, toss the strawberries with the balsamic vinegar. Mix well, cover, and refrigerate for 30 minutes.

2. Make the syrup. Meanwhile, in a medium saucepan, combine ½ cup water, the sugar, and lemon zest and simmer over medium heat until the sugar is completely dissolved. Remove the pan from the heat, cover it, and steep for at least 20 minutes.

3. Puree the strawberries. When the strawberries are done marinating, puree them in a food processor or blender, then strain the seeds out with a fine-mesh strainer to yield about 2 cups puree. Discard the seeds and transfer the puree to a large bowl.

4. Strain, cover, and chill the syrup. Strain the syrup into the strawberry puree, add the lemon juice, and whisk until combined. After covering the container, transfer it to an ice bath and let it cool for about 20 minutes to stop the cooking process. Chill for at least 4 hours.

Once the syrup is completely cold...

5. Dissolve the gelatin in ⅓ cup cold water. See page 15.

6. Spike the syrup with the cold champagne and gelatin mixture. See page 16.

7. Churn the sorbet for at least 20 minutes. See page 17.

8. Serve with freshly cracked black pepper, if desired.

RASPBERRY BELLINI

SORBET   *Traditionally Bellinis are made with prosecco, an Italian sparkling wine, and peach puree. However, a dear friend requested a raspberry Bellini sorbet, so here it is. Although prosecco is the traditional sparkling wine used, many restaurants and cocktail bars now make it with champagne as well, so feel free to do the same.*

⅔ cup water plus ⅓ cup cold water, divided

⅔ cup sugar

1 pound raspberries

2 tablespoons fresh lemon juice

½ packet (½ tablespoon) gelatin

1½ cups cold (refrigerated) prosecco or other sparkling wine

MAKES ABOUT 1 QUART

1 Make the syrup. In a medium saucepan, combine ⅔ cup water and the sugar and simmer over medium-low heat until the sugar is completely dissolved. Remove the pan from the heat and allow the syrup to cool.

2. Puree the raspberries. While the syrup cools, puree the raspberries in a food processor or blender, then strain through a fine-mesh strainer and discard the seeds. Transfer the puree to a large bowl.

3. Strain, cover, and chill the syrup. Strain the syrup into the raspberry puree, and stream in the lemon juice. Whisk until combined. After covering the container, transfer it to an ice bath and let it cool for about 20 minutes to stop the cooking process. Chill for at least 4 hours.

Once the syrup is completely cold...

4. **Dissolve the gelatin** in ⅓ cup cold water. See page 15.

5. **Spike the syrup** with the cold prosecco and gelatin mixture. See page 16.

6. **Churn the sorbet** for 15 minutes. See page 17. Warning: This sorbet aerates very quickly, so keep an eye on it and stop churning before it gets too fluffy.

BOOZY WHIPPED CREAM

MAKES ABOUT 1½ CUPS

While you can top your ice cream cocktail with classic whipped cream, just a couple tablespoons of liquor go a long way toward making sure your frozen treat is as sauced as possible.

Combine ½ cup cold heavy cream, 2 tablespoons liquor (brandy and Kahlúa are classic choices, but get creative), and ½ tablespoon sugar in a chilled medium bowl. Whisk gently until the sugar dissolves, then whisk more vigorously until the cream thickens and holds a shape.

MIMOSA

SORBET   *This brunch cocktail sorbet is lovely when allowed to harden in the freezer for a few hours, but it's even more divine straight out of the ice cream maker. If you open a fresh bottle of champagne for this sorbet, you can sometimes hear the champagne bubbles bursting while you scoop the finished product straight out of the freezer bowl and into a glass. Orange juice from a carton works just fine for this recipe, but fresh juice is best.*

½ cup water plus ⅓ cup cold water, divided

½ cup sugar

grated zest of 1 lemon

2 cups fresh orange juice

2 tablespoons fresh lemon juice

1 packet (1 tablespoon) gelatin

1½ cups cold (refrigerated) champagne

MAKES ABOUT 1 QUART

1 **Make the syrup.** In a medium saucepan, combine ½ cup water, the sugar, and lemon zest and simmer over low heat until the sugar is completely dissolved, about 5 minutes. Remove the pan from the heat, cover it, and steep for at least 20 minutes.

2. **Strain, cover, and chill the syrup.** Strain the syrup into the orange juice and lemon juice in a large bowl and whisk until combined. Chill for at least 4 hours.

Once the syrup is completely cold...

3. **Dissolve the gelatin** in ⅓ cup cold water. See page 15.

4. **Spike the syrup** with the cold champagne and gelatin mixture. See page 16.

5. **Churn the sorbet** for at least 20 minutes. See page 17.

WHISKEY CARAMEL SAUCE

MAKES A LITTLE MORE THAN 2 CUPS

Place 1½ cups sugar in a medium saucepan and add ½ cup water. Make sure the sides of the pan are clean. Stir slowly over low heat until the sugar is completely dissolved. As the sugar cooks, the caramel will thicken and become rich in color. Resist the urge to stir. Once it reaches the desired caramel color, turn off the heat.

Scald 1 cup heavy cream with 1 teaspoon vanilla extract (see page 11). Gradually stream the hot cream into the caramel while whisking. The caramel sauce will immediately bubble over, so carefully stir it until all the heavy cream is added.

Pour the caramel sauce into a container and refrigerate until cold, about 5 hours, then stir in 2 ounces Irish whiskey or to taste.

GIN AND JUICE

SHERBET   *Whoever thought of pairing the bitter sweetness of grapefruit juice with juniper-laden gin was a genius. The flavors come together with sweet orange juice to create a delicious sherbet that you can most certainly enjoy after a hearty brunch with friends. And it's a snap to put together.*

1 cup sugar

1⅓ cups fresh orange juice

⅔ cup fresh grapefruit juice

juice of 1 lime

¾ cup milk

¾ cup heavy cream

1 packet (1 tablespoon) gelatin

⅓ cup cold water

⅔ cup cold (refrigerated) gin

MAKES ABOUT 1 QUART

1 **Make the syrup.** Whisk the sugar, orange juice, grapefruit juice, and lime juice together in a large bowl until the sugar is completely dissolved.

2. **Whisk in the milk and heavy cream.**

3. **Cover and chill the syrup** for at least 4 hours. See page 14.

Once the syrup is completely cold...

4. **Dissolve the gelatin** in the cold water. See page 15.

5. **Spike the syrup** with the cold gin and gelatin mixture. See page 16.

6. **Churn the sherbet** for at least 20 minutes. See page 17.

VODKA WATERMELON GRANITA

GRANITA   *This recipe was inspired by the classic picnic tradition of vodka watermelon. But instead of cutting a hole in a watermelon and pouring a bottle of vodka in it to marinate, we chunked up the watermelon, poured enough vodka to cover it, and let it soak for a few days. We recommend marinating for at least 48 hours, but it will stay fresh refrigerated for about a week.*

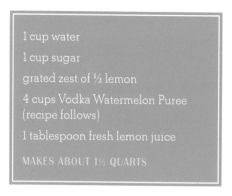

1 cup water

1 cup sugar

grated zest of ½ lemon

4 cups Vodka Watermelon Puree
(recipe follows)

1 tablespoon fresh lemon juice

MAKES ABOUT 1½ QUARTS

1 **Make the syrup.** Combine the water, sugar, and lemon zest in a small saucepan over high heat and bring to boil. When the syrup is boiling, remove the pan from the heat, cover it, and steep for 15 minutes, then allow to cool.

2. **Cover and chill the syrup** for at least 4 hours.

Once the syrup is completely cold...

3. **Mix the syrup** together with the watermelon puree and lemon juice. Pour into a shallow container.

4. **Freeze the granita** for 2 hours. Then run a fork through it to break up the ice that forms. Repeat every 30 minutes until you've reached your desired texture, about 2 hours longer.

VODKA WATERMELON PUREE

Look for a relatively small watermelon; a 6-pounder will do the job. It's likely you'll still have more watermelon flesh than needed. We recommend making the full recipe of puree and freezing the rest for other uses, such as Vodka Watermelon Sorbet (page 140). You should have enough puree for about three recipes.

4½ pounds chopped watermelon flesh

2 cups vodka, or as needed

MAKES ABOUT 3 QUARTS

1. Marinate the watermelon. Place the watermelon in a container and add enough vodka to cover. Allow to marinate in the refrigerator for at least 48 hours, or up to 1 week.

Once the watermelon has marinated...

2. Puree the watermelon and vodka. You may notice a white foam forming on top. Skim this off.

3. Strain the puree. Pour the puree through a strainer to remove all the seeds.

VODKA WATERMELON SORBET

SORBET   *This sorbet is heavy on the vodka and the flavor, but it churns out in a nice sophisticated, creamy texture.*

1 cup water plus ¼ cup cold water, divided

1 cup sugar

peel of 1 lemon

2 allspice berries

4 cups Vodka Watermelon Puree (page 139)

juice of 1 lemon

1 packet (1 tablespoon) gelatin

MAKES ABOUT 1 QUART

1. Make the syrup. In a medium saucepan, combine 1 cup water, the sugar, lemon peel, and allspice berries and simmer over medium heat until the sugar is completely dissolved, about 5 minutes. Remove the pan from the heat, cover, and allow the syrup to cool.

2. Strain, cover, and chill the syrup. Strain the syrup into the watermelon puree in a large bowl. Discard the lemon peel and allspice berries. Add the lemon juice and whisk until combined. After covering the container, transfer it to an ice bath for about 20 minutes to stop the cooking process, then transfer it to the refrigerator. Chill for at least 4 hours.

Once the syrup is completely cold...

3. Dissolve the gelatin in ¼ cup cold water. See page 15.

4. Add the gelatin. Transfer the cold syrup to a large bowl. Strain the gelatin into the syrup and whisk until thoroughly blended.

5. Churn the sorbet for at least 15 minutes. See page 17.

CHOCOLATE SAUCE

MAKES ABOUT 4 CUPS

In a medium saucepan over low heat, combine 9 ounces chopped dark chocolate (or dark chocolate chips), 2 cups water, 1 cup heavy cream, and ⅓ cup sugar. Bring to boil while whisking constantly. Simmer the sauce until it's thick and coats the back of a spoon or spatula, about 15 minutes. Note: Stay close while making this, as it can easily boil over.

Variation

WHISKEY CHOCOLATE SAUCE: To make a happy hour sundae extra tipsy, stir in ¼ cup whiskey after the sauce thickens.

SANGRIA

SORBET   *Wine—what's not to like? The combination and ratio of fruits used in this recipe are up to you. We suggest using a good-quality wine that you'd be willing to drink with a meal and your favorite firm fruits that can stand up to red wine. Good options are apples (skin on), tangerine (zest removed whole and reserved), orange (zest removed whole and reserved), diced pineapple, or kiwi (skin removed).*

1 (750 ml) bottle plus ½ cup dry red wine, such as syrah, divided

citrus zest (see note above)

1 cup sugar

½ cup chopped fruit (see note above)

½ cup grappa

1½ cups plus ⅓ cup cold soda water, or more

1 packet (1 tablespoon) gelatin

MAKES ABOUT 1 QUART

1 **Reduce the wine.** In a large saucepan, combine 1 bottle red wine, the citrus zest, and sugar and simmer over low heat until reduced to about half (about 16 ounces), 15 to 20 minutes. Don't worry about overreducing; it can be corrected in Step 5.

2. **Soak the fruit** in ½ cup red wine and refrigerate until cold.

3. **Strain, cover, and chill the reduced wine base.** Strain the reduced wine, which should be rich and sweet, similar to a port, and discard the citrus rind. Add the grappa. After covering the container, transfer it to an ice bath and let it cool for about 20 minutes to stop the cooking process. Chill for at least 4 hours.

Once the base is completely cold...

4. Add the soda water. Measure the red wine base and add enough cold soda water, about 1½ cups, to equal 4 cups total.

5. Strain the cold fruit and reserve the liquid. Set the fruit aside.

6. Dissolve the gelatin in the remaining ⅓ cup cold soda water. See page 15.

7. Add the gelatin. Pour the cold red wine base into a large bowl. Pour the gelatin into a medium bowl and whisk in the reserved fruit liquid until combined. Then whisk the gelatin mixture into the red wine base until thoroughly blended.

8. Churn the sorbet for at least 15 minutes. See page 17. Once the sorbet is the desired thickness, add the drained fruit to the ice cream maker and let it churn in.

Variation

WHITE SANGRIA: Omit the red wine and grappa. Substitute with a dry white wine such as a sauvignon blanc or pinot grigio. You can also add ¼ cup triple sec and ¼ cup brandy. For the fruit, try melon, orange slices, peaches, and/or raspberries.

GRAPEFRUIT FIZZ

SORBET   *This clean and crisp sorbet is perfect for awakening the taste buds.*

1 cup cold water, divided

⅔ cup sugar

grated zest of 2 limes

1 cup grapefruit juice

¼ cup lime juice

½ packet (½ tablespoon) gelatin

¼ cup cold (refrigerated) triple sec

1¼ cups cold (refrigerated) sparkling wine

MAKES ABOUT 1 QUART

1 **Make the syrup.** In a medium saucepan, combine ⅔ cup water and the sugar and lime zest and simmer until the sugar is dissolved, about 5 minutes. Remove the pan from the heat, cover, and steep for at least 20 minutes.

2. **Strain the syrup** into the grapefruit juice and lime juice in a large bowl and whisk until combined.

3. **Cover and chill the syrup** for at least 4 hours. See page 14. After covering the container, transfer it to an ice bath for about 20 minutes to stop the cooking process, then transfer it to the refrigerator.

Once the syrup is completely cold...

4. **Dissolve the gelatin** in the remaining ⅓ cup cold water. See page 15.

5. **Spike the syrup** with the cold triple sec, sparkling wine, and gelatin mixture. See page 16.

6. **Churn the sorbet** for at least 20 minutes. See page 17.

TIPSY
SUNDAES
AND FLOATS

MUDSLIDE SUNDAE

Family-centric restaurant chains may have turned the mudslide into a child's treat, but we've reclaimed it for the rowdier crowd. Vanilla, Kahlúa, and Bailey's Irish Cream ice creams make a fantastic trio for this sundae.

1 scoop Vanilla with Vodka ice cream (page 21)

1 scoop Coffee with Kahlúa ice cream (page 34)

1 scoop Irish Cream ice cream (page 84)

Chocolate Sauce (page 141)

cookie sticks, for garnish

1 **Assemble the sundae.** Stack the ice cream scoops in a tall glass. Drizzle with chocolate sauce and slide a cookie stick into the side of the glass so it looks like an old-school float.

SEX ON THE BEACH RAINBOW SHERBET

One of our personal favorite sweet treats, rainbow sherbet, gets drastically updated as a Sex on the Beach cocktail. Cranberry and vodka sherbet gets swirled with orange and vodka sherbet and a sweetened kick of peach Schnapps-infused sherbet.

As you may have guessed, this recipe requires using an ice cream maker three separate times. This means the freezer bowl must be washed and completely frozen before the next component is churned. It may be time-consuming, but think of it as three days' worth of foreplay before having Sex on the Beach.

⅓ quart Cape Cod sherbet (page 126)

⅓ quart Screwdriver sherbet (page 129)

⅓ quart Peach with Schnapps sherbet (page 65)

MAKES ABOUT 1 QUART

1 **Prepare the sherbets.** You can use one flavor right out of the machine, but the other two will probably have to be made ahead of time and stored in the freezer. Just allow them to soften up outside of the freezer for the last 5 minutes of churning the last flavor and you should be good to go.

2. **Marble the sherbets.** In a 1-quart container, layer about one-half of the most recently churned ice cream. Then scoop about one-half of the second flavor that has been softening up outside the freezer. Then add about one-half of the third flavor. Repeat the layering once more with the remaining ice cream. Return the marbled ice cream to the freezer to firm up for a few hours before serving.

IRISH SHOT IN AN IRISH BEER SUNDAE

The drink most commonly known as an Irish Car Bomb has been known to get people so easily sauced that they barely notice they're drunk until they wake up the next day. We took the classic Guinness, whiskey, and Bailey's combination and turned it into a sundae that you won't soon forget. Separately, the Guinness ice cream, which includes chocolate, and the Irish Cream ice cream are deliciously nuanced. Together, topped with Whiskey Caramel Sauce and Chocolate Sauce, they're a chocolate-laced symphony of flavors. Since there are two different ice creams required for the sundae, assuming you have only one freezer bowl, you might want to consider beginning this recipe three days before you plan to serve it.

1 scoop Guinness ice cream
(page 82)

1 scoop Irish Cream ice cream
(page 84)

Whiskey Caramel Sauce (page 136)

Chocolate Sauce (page 141)

shaved white chocolate, for garnish

MAKES 1 SERVING

1 **Assemble the sundae.** Place both ice cream scoops in a dish and top with caramel sauce and chocolate sauce. Garnish with shaved white chocolate.

HOT BUTTERED RUM FLOAT

This drink is perfect for the winter months when you may crave ice cream but want a bit of warmth.

1 teaspoon butter, at room temperature

1 teaspoon brown sugar

nutmeg

hot water

2 small scoops Buttered Rum ice cream (page 46)

MAKES 1 SERVING

1 Place the butter, brown sugar, and a dash of nutmeg in a mug and muddle gently.

2. Pour hot water about two-thirds of the way up the side of the mug. Add 1 scoop ice cream and stir to dissolve. Add the second scoop as a topper. Garnish with additional nutmeg, if desired. Serve immediately.

NOR'EASTER FLOAT

The Nor'easter has many interpretations in the cocktail world. Some use cranberry juice; some sweeten with just sugar. What they all have in common is the use of bourbon, that strong, woody-tasting whiskey that claims Kentucky as its homeland. This version comes from the restaurant Char No. 4 in Brooklyn, New York. Their ingenious use of maple syrup directly influenced our Maple with Bourbon ice cream.

2 ounces bourbon

splash of maple syrup

½ ounce fresh lime juice

splash of ginger beer

1 scoop Maple with Bourbon ice cream (page 54)

MAKES 1 SERVING

1 **Make the cocktail.** Combine the bourbon, maple syrup, and lime juice in a shaker with ice and shake well. Strain into a glass and add the ginger beer.

2. **Top with the ice cream** and serve immediately.

DARK AND STORMY FLOAT

This classic drink of ginger beer, rum, and bitters gets a sweet little kick with the addition of Caramel with Spiced Rum ice cream.

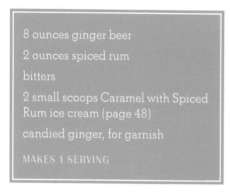

8 ounces ginger beer

2 ounces spiced rum

bitters

2 small scoops Caramel with Spiced Rum ice cream (page 48)

candied ginger, for garnish

MAKES 1 SERVING

1 Pour the ginger beer into a glass, then add the spiced rum and mix. Add 2 to 3 drops bitters.

2. **Add the ice cream.** Add 1 scoop of ice cream to the glass and allow it to dissolve. Place the second scoop on top and sprinkle with candied ginger, if using. Serve immediately.

BAR BRAWL ICE CREAM SANDWICH

As the name implies, this treat was inspired by a rowdy night out at a dive bar. Vanilla with Bourbon ice cream and Chocolate with Irish Whiskey ice cream are swirled together, covered in pretzels, and sandwiched between two Guinness gingerbread cookies shaped like coasters.

This treat takes some planning, depending on whether you have more than one freezer bowl for your ice cream maker. You'll need ½ quart each chocolate and vanilla ice creams. They're made separately and then layered together in a container so they can freeze to a firmer texture. You may need to plan 2 days in advance, but the wow factor at a party makes it worth it. If you don't want to bother with the gingerbread coasters, you can always just serve the ice cream with broken pretzels on top.

½ quart Vanilla with Bourbon ice cream (page 21)

½ quart Chocolate with Irish Whiskey ice cream (page 23)

24 Guinness Gingerbread Coasters (recipe follows)

1 cup, or more, pretzel pieces

MAKES ABOUT 12 ICE CREAM SANDWICHES

1 Prepare the ice cream. You can use one flavor right out of the machine, but the second flavor will probably have to be made ahead of time and stored in the freezer. Just allow it to soften outside the freezer for the last 10 minutes of churning the second flavor and you should be good to go.

2. Marble the ice creams. In a 1-quart container, layer about one-third of the vanilla ice cream, then add about one-third of the chocolate ice cream. Repeat the layers twice more with the remaining ice cream. Allow the newly marbled ice cream to firm up in the freezer for a few hours.

Once the marbled ice cream is frozen...

2. Assemble the sandwiches. Place 1 cookie on a serving plate or your work surface. Sprinkle with pretzel bits, add 1 scoop of the marbled ice cream, sprinkle more pretzel bits, and add a second cookie on top. Repeat with the remaining cookies. Serve immediately.

GUINNESS GINGERBREAD COASTERS

The key to making these Guinness gingerbread cookies look like coasters is the cookie cutter. We use the mouth of a pint glass to make the round. Once the cookies are on the baking sheet, lightly grease the bottom of the glass and simply press it onto the center of each cookie before putting the cookie sheet in the oven.

1 (12-ounce) bottle Guinness Extra Stout

2½ cups flour

½ teaspoon baking powder

½ teaspoon baking soda

¼ teaspoon salt

1 teaspoon ground cinnamon

½ teaspoon ground nutmeg

½ teaspoon ground allspice

½ teaspoon ground cloves

1½ teaspoons ground ginger

½ cup unsalted butter, at room temperature

1 cup brown sugar

⅓ cup molasses

1 egg

MAKES ABOUT 24 COOKIES

1. Reduce the Guinness. In a small saucepan over low heat, simmer the Guinness until reduced by about half, about 25 minutes. Set aside.

2. Sift together the flour, baking powder, baking soda, salt, cinnamon, nutmeg, allspice, cloves, and ginger in a medium bowl.

3. Cream the butter and sugar together in a large bowl until light in color. Beat in the molasses, egg, and ⅓ cup of the reduced Guinness.

4. Fold the flour mixture into the butter mixture until combined.

5. Chill the dough. Divide the dough in half and pat each half into a disk. Completely wrap each one in plastic wrap and refrigerate for at least 3 hours, or up to 48 hours.

Once the dough is cold...

6. Preheat the oven to 350°F and line a cookie sheet with parchment paper.

7. Roll out the dough. On a floured surface, roll out each disk of dough to about ⅛ inch thick. Cut out the cookies using the mouth of a pint glass, or a round cookie cutter.

8. Place the cookies on the prepared cookie sheet. Lightly grease the bottom of the pint glass and gently press it onto each cookie to make an impression.

9. Bake the cookies until they look dry but are soft to the touch, 10 to 12 minutes. Allow to cool completely on wire racks.

10. For ice cream sandwiches, freeze the cookies before assembling the sandwiches. It prevents the ice cream from melting too quickly.

CONVERSIONS

MEASURE	EQUIVALENT	METRIC
1 teaspoon		5 milliliters
1 tablespoon	3 teaspoons	14.8 milliliters
1 cup	16 tablespoons	236.8 milliliters
1 pint	2 cups	473.6 milliliters
1 quart	4 cups	947.2 milliliters
1 liter	4 cups + 3 tablespoons	1000 milliliters
1 ounce (dry)	2 tablespoons	28.35 grams
1 pound	16 ounces	453.49 grams
2.21 pounds	35.3 ounces	1 kilogram
270°F / 350°F		132°C / 177°C

ABOUT THE AUTHORS

VALERIE LUM was born and reared in Sacramento, California. After earning her bachelors degree in journalism from California State University of Chico, she embarked on a career as a reporter covering small towns in California and Oklahoma. On a whim, she moved to New York City where she continues her work as a writer and cook. When she's not attempting to burn off the ice cream poundage from this book by running, she can be found making brownies, blondies, and cookies as the baker at Bierkraft in Park Slope, Brooklyn, and in the kitchen of her tiny Brooklyn apartment where she cooks for her family and friends.

JENISE ADDISON was born and reared in Corona, Queens, and has had a love for good food and honest ways to make it since childhood. After attending Long Island City High School, majoring in restaurant driven culinary education, she went on to attend the French Culinary Institute with a little help from celebrity chef Bobby Flay and aid of the inspiring organization Careers through Culinary Arts Programs, which helps high school students break into the demanding culinary world. Jenise now spends her time brining, curing, butchering, and fermenting at Bierkraft in Brooklyn.